PREDICTING
NUCLEAR AND OTHER
TECHNOLOGICAL DISASTERS

PREDICTING NUCLEAR AND OTHER TECHNOLOGICAL DISASTERS

CHRISTOPHER LAMPTON

Franklin Watts ▪ 1989
New York ▪ *London* ▪ *Toronto* ▪ *Sydney*

Diagrams by Vantage Art

Photographs courtesy: Gamma Liaison: p. 8 (Pablo Bartholemew);
Sovfoto: p. 10 (Tass); Photo Researchers: pp. 63 (Michael Sullivan),
75 (both) (insert) (Paolo Koch), (center) (John W. Schults), 84
(Kenneth Murray), 131, (top) (Dr. Tony Brain); Center for Disease
Control: p. 133, (bottom); UPI/Bettmann: pp. 66, 72, 105, 107.

Library of Congress Cataloging-in-Publication Data

Lampton, Christopher.
Predicting nuclear and other technological disasters.

Bibliography: p.
Includes index.
Summary: Discusses risks involved in state-of-the-
art technology and what we can do to make the risks less
and prevent disasters such as Three Mile Island,
Chernobyl, and Bhopal.
1. Technology—Risk assessment—Juvenile literature.
2. Nuclear power plants—Risk assessment—Juvenile
literature. [1. Technology—Risk assessment.
2. Nuclear power plants—Risk assessment] I. Title.
T174.5.L35   1989   363.1   89-9160
ISBN 0-531-10784-1

CONTENTS

PREDICTING

NUCLEAR AND OTHER TECHNOLOGICAL DISASTERS

Union Carbide plant in Bhopal, India, where a leak of methyl isocyanate— a substance used in the preparation of commercial pesticides—killed approximately 2,000 people in December 1984.

PREDICTING

INTRODUCTION

RISKY SYSTEMS

NEWS FLASH—*An accidental release of poison gases from a chemical plant in Bhopal, India, killed at least 2,000 people this morning. . . . Some of the victims ran choking and screaming through the streets; others died in their sleep. . . . Corpses are piled on the sidewalks awaiting disposal. . . . Ten thousand people are crammed into a hospital with only a thousand beds. . . . The incident is already being termed the worst chemical industrial accident of modern times. . . .*

NEWS FLASH—*An explosion in a nuclear reactor this morning at Chernobyl in the Ukraine has claimed an as yet unknown number of victims. . . . Increased radioactivity has been detected in Eastern Europe. . . . There is a possibility of thousands of additional deaths from cancer over the next twenty to*

View of Unit 4 (arrow) of the Chernobyl nuclear power plant in the Soviet Union. A meltdown crippled the unit in May 1986.

thirty years. . . . Evidence shows that the most cat-
astrophic type of nuclear accident may have taken
place—a reactor core meltdown. . . .

■ ■ ■

Human beings are technological creatures. We make
tools, and with those tools we shape the world in
which we live.

Technology protects us from the extremes of our
environment. Unlike our distant forebears, we need
not fear the freezing cold of winter because we have
centrally heated houses to keep us warm. Great
distances mean little to us; we speed across them in
automobiles, trains, and airplanes. Medical science
protects us from many diseases that were once commonly fatal.

Any kind of tool, no matter how simple, can be
considered technology. A lever, for instance, is technology, as is a wedge or a wheel. As our ability to
create tools has become more sophisticated, however,
our technology has increasingly taken the form of
systems—collections of parts, or components, that
work together for a common purpose. A wristwatch is
a technological system, as is an automobile, a television set, and a nuclear power plant. In fact, a system
as complex as a nuclear power plant is not made of
simple components; rather, it is made up of *subsystems*, which are complete technological systems in
themselves.

Any technological system can fail. The failure of a
system is always undesirable, but the failure of some
systems is less desirable than that of others. In
extreme cases, the failure of a technological system
can result in death, loss of property, and even large-
scale destruction. Such failures can properly be

termed "technological disasters" because they result from the malfunction of a technological system.

The failure of a simple technological system, such as a wristwatch, could hardly be termed a disaster. At worst, such a failure might make you late for work or school, an outcome that could be considered undesirable but hardly catastrophic. The failure of an automobile, on the other hand, could have considerably more dire results—if the brakes fail while the car is approaching a busy intersection, for instance. And the failure of a nuclear power plant has the potential to kill thousands of people, as we shall see.

A technological system with the potential to cause death and injury to human beings is sometimes called a *risky system*. Why do we allow such systems to exist? Usually, because the lack of such a system is even riskier than having the system itself. A furnace, for instance, is a risky system, because a failure of the furnace system could set a house on fire and injure or kill its occupants. But the absence of a furnace is riskier still, because the occupants of an unheated house are more likely to die of pneumonia than the occupants of a heated house are to die in a fire.

As long as we live in a technological society, we will live with risky systems. It is important, then, that we be able to predict what events will cause the failure of such systems and try to prevent these events from happening—or, at the very least, minimize the undesirable effects of such failures when they occur. Furthermore, it is important that we have some way to assess just how risky a system is, so that we can decide whether the risk of having the system is greater than the risk of not having it—or whether it's worth the trouble and expense of replacing the risky system with one less risky.

Alas, there is no magic crystal ball that will tell us that such-and-such a system will fail at such-and-such a time on such-and-such a date. The best we can do is calculate the probability of such a failure. Such a calculation is called a *probabilistic risk analysis*, PRA for short. It can, in theory, tell us exactly the degree of danger associated with a particular risky system.

Do such calculations actually work? This is a subject of considerable controversy. Many people, especially those who advocate the introduction of more and more complex technological systems, believe that risk analysis is a fairly exact science, that we can make reasonably accurate calculations about the risk involved in these systems. Others, especially those who believe that technology has grown too complex for human beings to manage, believe that risk analysis is not only inaccurate but dangerous, because it gives us the illusion that we understand the dangers of our technology.

Which side is right? It may be too early to tell. In this book, we'll introduce you to the methods of risk analysis, then take a look at three risky systems and the risks associated with them: nuclear-energy technology, chemical-processing technology, and biotechnology.

The technology that we will study in greatest detail is nuclear energy, not because it is necessarily the riskiest of these technologies but because it is the one in which risk analysis has been carried to its most advanced levels. We'll also discuss technological disasters that have already occurred, including the failure of nuclear reactors at Three Mile Island in the United States and Chernobyl in the Soviet Union, and the chemical disaster in Bhopal, India, that killed thousands of people.

Finally, we will ask whether these technologies are worth the risk. However, this is a question that can be answered only by you, the technological creature reading this book.

PART ONE
PROBABILISTIC RISK ANALYSIS

PREDICTING

ONE
PROBABILITY

Is it possible to predict the future . . . perfectly? Can we know tomorrow's weather down to the last wisp of cloud in the sky? Can we predict the rise and fall of the Dow Jones average to the last decimal point? Can we foretell the winner of the World Series (or the presidential election) in the year 1996?

You might think that such a thing is possible—at least in theory. By using our knowledge of the present, and of the way in which certain causes tend to follow certain effects, we should be able to extrapolate from the events of today to the events of tomorrow and predict those events with a precision that would make a weather forecaster blush.

In practice, however, we are not able to do this—and we never will be. The reason that perfect prediction of the future isn't possible is that it would require perfect knowledge of the present, and there's no way we can get that. We would have to know the position of every atom—in fact, the position of every subatomic particle—in the universe, the directions in which those particles are headed, and the speed and momentum with which they are headed there. Then we would have to program all of that information into a superpowerful computer that would then calculate where all of those particles would be tomorrow or next year or twenty years from now.

Alas, the very laws of physics tell us that such knowledge is not possible, even if we had perfect measuring instruments at our disposal. And, even if it were, a computer that could hold so much information about the universe would need to be larger than the universe itself—a logical contradiction. You would think that we could get by with just the information about the position and momentum of particles on the Planet Earth, since this is where most of the human future will be taking place, at least for the next decade or two. But the weather on earth is driven by energy that travels millions of miles through space from the sun. And, as we will see in Chapter Five, a small percentage of all cases of cancer on earth are caused by particles that shoot into our atmosphere from outer space, propelled to tremendous speeds by explosions in distant stars and galaxies. Thus, life on earth is profoundly influenced by events taking place many millions of miles, even millions of light-years, away.

A prediction of the future based on perfect knowledge and the way in which one event inevitably follows another is called a *deterministic prediction*, because it assumes that the events of the future are precisely determined by the events of the present. Deterministic prediction is seductive; we've all seen cause-and-effect relationships between present and future in action. If you set up a row of dominoes on a table in such a way that each domino will knock over the next domino if it falls, you can be virtually certain that knocking over the first domino will eventually result in the knocking over of the last domino, though there may be hundreds or even thousands of dominoes in between. This is a deterministic prediction, because we are saying that the knocking over of the last domino is determined by the knocking over of the first.

And yet there is a small possibility that knocking over the first domino will *not* result in knocking over the last. What if your best friend decides to hold the last domino in place, so that it cannot fall, or removes the dominoes from the center of the row so that the dominoes to both sides of the gap cannot come into contact? Or what if a nuclear weapon, launched as part of a war that has nothing to do with your domino experiments, annihilates your home and turns the last domino to dust before it can topple over? Such events are unlikely, but they are not impossible. They represent a small but significant uncertainty in your ability to predict the future of the dominoes.

Few things in the real world are as predictable as dominoes. To paraphrase the Scottish poet Robert Burns, the best-laid plans of mice and men often go astray . . . and usually through no fault of the mice or the men. You may think that programming the VCR to record your favorite television show will inevitably result in a fresh new videotape that you can watch tomorrow morning. But what if the power fails during the afternoon, and the VCR loses its programming, or your mother decides to reprogram it to record *her* favorite show?

External events are always intervening in our predictions of the future, which makes deterministic prediction a risky business, indeed. The candidate who looks to be the overwhelming favorite to win next month's election may lose because of unexpected revelations about his or her financial dealings. The company whose stock looks to be a sure money-maker may turn out to be a loser when their product proves to be unreliable.

Is it impossible, then, to know anything about the future? Is there an opaque wall between today and tomorrow that will prevent us from ever knowing what will happen beyond the present moment?

No. If this were true, there would be no such thing as weather forecasts. We would have no way of knowing if the next day, or even the upcoming afternoon, held rain or sun, calm or storm. Of course, weather forecasts aren't always correct, not precisely speaking, anyway. We've all known the frustration of being told that the next day's weather would probably be sunny, only to find our planned picnic drowned in unexpected rain.

The key word, though, is "probably." Weather forecasts are rarely deterministic; instead, they are couched in terms of *probabilities*. We are rarely told that it will definitely rain tomorrow morning; instead, we are told that there is an 80 percent probability of rain. If it doesn't rain, we can't say that the forecast was wrong—just that it was misleading. An 80 percent probability of rain, after all, is also a 20 percent probability of no rain. If it fails to rain four out of every five times that we are told there is an 80 percent probability of rain, then we can say that the forecasts were wrong, but then only in a general sense. No specific forecast will have been incorrect. In fact, it *should* fail to rain one out of every five times that we are told that there is an 80 percent probability of rain.

The difference between deterministic prediction and probabilistic prediction is that deterministic prediction says that Event A *will* be followed by Event B, while probabilistic prediction states the *probability* that Event A will be followed by Event B. When we say that the toppling of the last domino is certain to follow the toppling of the first domino, we are making a deterministic prediction; if we say that the last domino has a 99 percent probability of toppling after the first domino has toppled, we are making a probabilistic prediction.

In general, probabilistic predictions are based on *observed frequencies*—that is, someone has observed the predicted sequence of events taking place in the past and has noted how likely it is to occur again. For instance, if you observed a hundred domino sequences and noted that in ninety-nine of them the toppling of the first domino was followed by the toppling of the last domino, then you would be justified in saying that there was a 99 percent probability—that is, ninety-nine chances out of a hundred—of this happening. Weather forecasters have observed that certain weather events have a certain probability of being followed by certain other weather events, and they base their forecasts on these probabilities.

You might wonder just what advantage there is to probabilistic prediction over deterministic prediction. After all, neither one gives us a clear picture of the future. Is an incorrect deterministic prediction any worse than a probabilistic prediction of an event that defies the odds?

There are two main advantages to probabilistic prediction. The first is that it gives us a measure of just how uncertain the prediction is. For instance, if we were told that it might rain tomorrow or it might be clear, we would be unsure of whether to schedule a picnic. On the other hand, if we are told that there is a 10 percent probability of rain tomorrow (and, therefore, a 90 percent probability that it will be clear), we might decide to go ahead with the picnic despite the relatively small uncertainty in the weather. But if we are told that there is a 50 percent probability of rain tomorrow (and, therefore, a 50 percent probability that it will be clear), we might decide that the uncertainty is too great and cancel the picnic. The probabilistic prediction allows us to assess the chance of rain and make our decision based on the probabilities.

The second advantage is that probabilistic prediction allows us to compare the risks of alternative choices. If we have a choice of building two technological systems, for instance, and are told that the first system has a 20 percent probability of failure and the second system has a 1 percent probability of failing, then we will almost certainly go with the second system, all other things being equal. Deterministic prediction, on the other hand, would merely show us that there were certain sequences of events that would lead to the failure of each system, but would give us no idea how likely these sequences were. The deterministic prediction would give us no basis for comparing the two systems.

In this chapter and the three that follow, we will look at methods that have been developed for predicting future events—especially the failure of technological systems—using probabilistic methods. Then we will see how such methods have actually been applied in predicting the disastrous failure of systems such as nuclear power plants.

· · ·

How do we assess the probability that an event will take place? Usually, through observation. If we observe that a certain event follows another event four times out of five, we know that the probability of the second event following the first is 80 percent.

With relatively simple events, however, we can predict the probability of certain outcomes without making a single observation, based on the nature of the events themselves. The classic example of a simple, predictable event is the tossing of a coin.

A coin has two sides, which we usually designate "heads" and "tails." If we toss the coin into the air, giving it a spin as we do so, it is as likely to come down with the heads side up as with the tails side up (unless, of course, someone has given us a coin that has two heads, or one that has been weighted so that one side tends to come up more often than the other). To calculate the probability of each of these events, we divide 100 (the maximum percentage) by 2 (the number of possible outcomes for the event), like this:

$$100 / 2 = 50$$

Thus, we say that when we toss a coin—an honest coin—we have a 50 percent probability of tossing heads and a 50 percent probability of tossing tails. We know this even without observing, say, 100 coin tosses and counting the number that come up heads and the number that come up tails. If you *did* observe 100 coin tosses, however, you would probably find that the number of tails and number of heads were very close to 50 each, though you might also get 49 heads and 51 tails, 53 heads and 47 tails, or something similar. You would rarely get *precisely* 50 percent of each, but you would always be somewhere in the vicinity. The more coins you toss, the closer you will get to a 50–50 split.

Once we know the probability of tossing heads on a single flip of the coin, we can then predict somewhat more complex sequences of events, using simple arithmetic. For instance, we can now predict that there is a 25 percent probability that you will toss two heads in a row.

How do we know this? When we toss a single coin, we know that there are two possible results, heads and tails. When we toss two coins, there are four possible results, as follows:

Coin 1—HEADS Coin 2—TAILS
Coin 1—TAILS Coin 2—HEADS
Coin 1—HEADS Coin 2—HEADS
Coin 1—TAILS Coin 2—TAILS

Since each of these results is equally likely, and since only one of these results involves two heads, we can determine the probability of tossing two heads by dividing 100 (the maximum percentage) by 4 (the number of events), like this:

$$100 / 4 = 25$$

Thus, the probability of tossing two heads in a row is 25 percent.

There is another way that we could calculate this. We could multiply the probability of flipping heads on the first coin by the probability of flipping heads on the second coin, like this:

$$50\% \times 50\% = 25\%$$

(You might wonder why multiplying 50 by 50 should produce a result of 25. Bear in mind that 50 percent is equivalent to the fraction .50, and thus we are multiplying .50 × .50, which produces a result of .25, or 25 percent.)

Why should multiplying the probabilities of two events by one another give us the probability that both events will take place? Because each of the two events occurs independently of the other. The tossing of the first coin doesn't affect the odds on the second. If there is a one-out-of-two chance that the first coin will come up heads, there is still a one-out-of-two chance that the second will not—even if the first one does. Thus, there is only one chance out of four that the second event *and* the first event will take place. In Chapter Three, we will see how the flipping of a coin can be drawn as a special kind of diagram called an *event tree* that will make this process clearer.

Similarly, we can use the same two methods to calculate the odds that we will toss *three* heads in a row. First, we can look at all the possible combinations of three coins, like this:

Coin 1—HEADS	Coin 2—HEADS	Coin 3—HEADS
Coin 1—HEADS	Coin 2—HEADS	Coin 3—TAILS
Coin 1—HEADS	Coin 2—TAILS	Coin 3—HEADS
Coin 1—HEADS	Coin 2—TAILS	Coin 3—TAILS
Coin 1—TAILS	Coin 2—HEADS	Coin 3—HEADS
Coin 1—TAILS	Coin 2—HEADS	Coin 3—TAILS
Coin 1—TAILS	Coin 2—TAILS	Coin 3—HEADS
Coin 1—TAILS	Coin 2—TAILS	Coin 3—TAILS

We can see that there are eight possible combinations of three coins. Therefore, we can calculate the odds on a single one of these combinations—three heads in a row—by dividing 100 by 8, like this:

$$100 / 8 = 12.5$$

Thus, we can say that the probability of tossing three heads in a row is 12.5 percent.

When we look at all possible outcomes of a sequence of events like this, we are said to be looking at what mathematicians call the *event space* for that sequence. The event space—which isn't a "space" at all, in the way we normally use the term—is simply the set of all possible sequences. The event space for a sequence of tossed coins gets very large very fast, as the sequence of tosses grows more complex. For instance, there are sixteen possible ways in which you can toss four coins, thirty-two possible ways in which you can toss five coins, sixty-four possible ways that you can toss six coins, and so on. This makes it rather awkward to write out the complete event space for these sequences, and we will not be doing so here.

The second way to calculate the probability of tossing three heads in a row is to multiply the odds on each toss by one another, like this:

$$50\% \times 50\% \times 50\% = 12.5\%$$

(Bear in mind, once again, that 50 percent is equivalent to .50 and that 12.5 percent is equivalent to .125.) This is somewhat easier than writing out the entire event space, though sometimes it is still necessary to do the latter.

The percentage of the event space that a given event occupies is the same as the probability that the event will occur. In the last example, three heads in a row occupies 1/8, or 12.5 percent, of the event space for the tossing of three coins. Therefore, it has a 12.5 percent chance of happening in a given set of three tosses.

In the tossing of coins, each event occupies the same percentage of the event space. Thus, tossing three tails in a row, or tossing heads followed by tails followed by heads, each has a 12.5 percent probability of occurring. But suppose the coin were weighted so that it had a greater chance of coming up heads than tails? Then certain events would occupy a greater percentage of the event space than other events. We can still calculate those percentages through ordinary arithmetic, though. Here's an example:

If, by observation, we determine that a weighted coin has a 60 percent chance of coming up heads and a 40 percent chance of coming up tails, then the probability of tossing two heads in a row would no longer be 25 percent. It would be:

$$60\% \times 60\% = 36\%$$
$$(.60 \times .60 = .36)$$

Thus, we would have a 36 percent chance of tossing two heads in a row. The event space for two tosses of the weighted coin would look like this:

Coin 1—HEADS   Coin 2—HEADS
(60% × 60% =) 36% probability
Coin 1—HEADS   Coin 2—TAILS
(60% × 40% =) 24% probability
Coin 1—TAILS   Coin 2—HEADS
(40% × 40% =) 16% probability
Coin 1—TAILS   Coin 2—TAILS
(40% × 60% =) 24% probability

The sequence of two heads in a row now occupies a greater percentage of the event space than any of the other possible sequences. There is a 36 percent probability that you will toss two heads in a row with the weighted coin. (On the other hand, there is still a 64 percent probability you will *not* toss two heads in a row, the sum of *all* the other sequences in the event space.) Similarly, there is now a 21.6 percent chance that you will flip *three* heads in a row, instead of a 12.5 percent chance.

As long as we are only talking about tossed coins, this information does us little practical good. Calculating probabilities by studying an event space, or by multiplying probabilities together, would seem at best an interesting but useless preoccupation.

However, it can actually become quite useful—the moment we bring in the concept of risk.

PREDICTING

TWO

RISK

It's reasonable to ask what good it does to be able to predict the outcome of a coin toss or a sequence of tosses. Here's one answer to that question:

Suppose you and a friend are betting on the outcome of a sequence of tosses. Since betting money is illegal in most states, we'll assume that you're betting baseball cards. You might bet one baseball card against three of your friend's baseball cards that you can toss two heads in a row (with an honest coin, of course). If you did this enough times, you would wind up with about as many baseball cards as you started out with, because you have one chance in four (or 25 percent) of tossing two coins in a row.

On the other hand, if you bet one baseball card against *two* of your friend's, then you will probably end up with fewer baseball cards than you started out with. And if you bet one baseball card against *four* of your friend's, you will probably end up with *more* than you started with. Thus, knowing the odds on tossing two heads in a row helps you to figure out how many baseball cards to bet. And, in fact, the laws of probability were roughly worked out by gamblers many centuries ago, before mathematicians ever discovered them.

Here's a second answer to the question, What good is predicting probabilities?

Suppose that someone told you that they would give you a very great treasure—millions of dollars, say, or a chest full of gold—if you flip a coin and it comes up heads. You would probably accept the offer—and the 50 percent chance of becoming rich. But suppose they told you that if the coin came up tails, they would pull out a gun and shoot you. That puts a different complexion on the offer. Is a 50 percent chance of getting rich worth a 50 percent chance of being killed? Probably not. It's a good bet (to put it in probabilistic terms) that you wouldn't accept this offer.

But suppose they told you that you could flip the coin three times and that all you had to do to win the treasure was to NOT toss three heads in a row. You would only be shot if you DID toss three heads in a row. This offer gives you an 87.5 percent chance of getting the treasure and only a 12.5 percent chance of being killed. Would you take the offer now? Probably not—but you might think twice about it.

What if the number of coin tosses was increased, so the point where you had a 99.999 percent probability of winning the treasure and only a .001 percent chance of being shot? You would probably accept the offer, because the probability that you would be killed is now so infinitesimally small that you can effectively disregard it. (Of course, you might still feel a little tense until the first time the coin came up tails.) You would be willing to accept the *risk* in order to gain the benefit.

Risk can be defined as the probability that a sequence of events will lead to a bad outcome. In our treasure scenario, the bad outcome would be the probability of getting shot.

In a sense, our treasure scenario is a kind of risky system, where each toss of the coin represents a component of the system. When we calculate the odds on a bad outcome—in this case, the tossing of several heads in a row, resulting in death—we are performing a *risk analysis* (or *risk assessment*) on the system. This risk analysis, in turn, helps us to decide whether we wish to accept the risks of the system in order to receive the benefits.

In real life, risk assessments are a great deal more complicated than this. It is immediately obvious that a system in which you will be killed for tossing heads on a single coin is riskier than a system in which you will be killed for tossing heads on each of three coins. But it is not immediately obvious whether it is riskier to produce electricity by burning coal or by pumping water through a cluster of radioactive rods. To give you a somewhat better feel for the complexity of risk assessment, let's devise a more complicated variation on our treasure scenario.

■ ■ ■

Imagine that you need money very badly. The Mafia is about to foreclose on a loan they made you six months earlier. (Unfortunately, you spent the loan buying baseball cards to support your gambling habit.) In desperation, you find two men, each of whom is willing to give you a valuable treasure under certain risky circumstances.

The first man requires that you flip a coin five times. If it comes up heads each time, you will be shot; otherwise, you will receive a valuable treasure. The second man requires that you roll three dice. If all three dice come up sixes, you will be shot; otherwise you will receive a valuable treasure.

Since you are desperate for money, you don't have the option of turning down both offers. Instead, you decide to accept the offer that involves less risk. But which offer is the less risky? Are you less likely to toss five heads in a row than to roll sixes on three dice? Instinctively, you might think that flipping five coins is less risky than rolling three dice, because it involves more events. But this isn't necessarily so.

To assess the risks of the two systems, we must first determine the probability of an undesirable outcome from each, then compare the probabilities. Using the principles that we discussed in the previous chapter, this isn't terribly difficult.

You'll recall that the probability of tossing heads on a single flip of the coin is 50 percent. Therefore, the probability of tossing heads five times in a row is

$$50\% \times 50\% \times 50\% \times 50\% \times 50\% = 3.125\%$$
$$(.50 \times .50 \times .50 \times .50 \times .50 = .03125)$$

The risk that you will be killed in the first system—the coin-tossing system—is 3.125 percent.

What are the risks of the dice-rolling system? First, we need to know the probability of rolling a six on a single die. There are six sides to a die, and each side has an equal probability of coming up on a single roll, assuming that the die hasn't been weighted. We can calculate the probability by dividing 100 by 6, like this:

$$100 \div 6 = 16.6666666 \ldots$$

For our purposes, it's okay to round this number off and say that we have a 16.6 percent chance of getting a six on a single roll of the die. To calculate the odds of rolling three sixes in a row, we multiply the odds on each roll by one another, like this:

$$16.6\% \times 16.6\% \times 16.6\% = .4574296\%$$
$$(.166 \times .166 \times .166 = .00457496)$$

Rounding this off, we can say that there is roughly a .457 percent chance of rolling three sixes in a row—and thus a .457 percent chance of being killed with the second system, or a bit less than half a percent. (This number is not quite accurate, because we have been rounding off our digits, but it is still close to half a percent.)

Now that we know the risks of both systems, we can see that the second system, with a risk of half a percent, is less risky than the first system, with a risk of more than 3 percent. Therefore you take the second man's offer, knowing that you have a much better chance of getting the treasure and a much lower chance of dying. Of course, it is always possible that, despite the odds, you will roll three sixes and be shot. But there is less chance of your being shot with the second system than with the first, and you are probably better off taking either risk than trying to pay off the Mafia with baseball cards.

■ ■ ■

How does this relate to the risk assessment of technological systems? Like our coin-tossing and dice-rolling systems, a technological system is made up of several components (the tosses or rolls), each of which has a certain probability of failing (coming up heads or sixes) and each of which must fail in order for the entire system to fail. Just as we multiply the probabilities together to calculate the probability of tossing multiple heads or rolling multiple sixes, so we multiply the probabilities of component failures together to get the probability of a total system failure.

To show how this works, we'll invent a simple technological system that we'll call the *Morning Wake-up System*. This is the system that gets you up in the morning so that you can go to school or work. The main portion of this system is a windup alarm clock that you have owned for several years. Every night before you go to bed, you set the clock to wake you up at 7:00 A.M. From previous experience, you know that the clock has a 5 percent chance of failing on any given night. However, you have arranged for several *backup systems* to awaken you in the event that the clock fails. If the alarm doesn't ring, your mother will come to your room and push you off the bed. If your mother doesn't appear and he doesn't hear from you by 7:10, your friend Al will telephone you. If Al doesn't phone, you may still wake up in time naturally, without any help. (This last backup system has a high failure rate; fortunately, it is rarely needed.)

In order for the Morning Wake-up System to fail, all of these subsystems—the small systems that make up the larger system—must fail. Under normal circumstances, these backup subsystems are unnecessary, or *redundant,* but if the main subsystem—the alarm clock—fails, they will be the only thing standing between you and oversleeping, which could have disastrous consequences at school or work.

The simultaneous failure of all four of these systems is analogous to tossing heads four times in a row, and we calculate the probability of such a failure in exactly the same way, by multiplying together the probabilities of the individual failures. Let's assume that, through experience, we know that each of the backup systems has the following probability of failing on a given morning:

Mom waking you up: 19%

Al telephoning: 46%

Waking up spontaneously: 98%

We can therefore calculate that the probability of a total system failure is:

$$5\% \times 19\% \times 46\% \times 98\% = .428\%$$

Thus, while each individual "component system" in the Morning Wake-up System has a fairly high probability of failing during the course of a year, the overall system has a fairly low probability of failing: only .428 percent. This is because the failure probability for any component system is fractional, that is, less than 100 percent. Thus, when the failure probabilities are multiplied together, they produce a small number, as fractions always do when multiplied together. This is a characteristic of *redundant systems*—that is, systems with backup component systems that take over when the main component systems fail. Systems with redundant parts always have a lower probability of failing than equivalent systems without redundant parts. By building this redundancy into a system, we decrease the risk of the system.

■ ■ ■

We can calculate the risk of large technological systems such as nuclear power plants just as we calculate the risks of your Morning Wake-up System, by determining the probability of failure for component parts or component systems and adding or multiplying those probabilities to determine the probability of total system failure. But these systems are so complicated that it is sometimes necessary to draw a picture, or diagram, to show how the risk of one component failure relates to the risk of another component failure. One type of diagram used to explore system failures is the *event tree,* which we will discuss in the next chapter.

PREDICTING

THREE

EVENT TREES

An event tree is a way of drawing the event space for a technological system so that you can find all sequences of events that lead to undesirable outcomes. By multiplying together the probabilities of the events occurring in each sequence, you can then determine the probability that any particular undesirable sequence will take place. This sounds terribly complicated, but it really isn't. An illustration should clear things up. Figure 3.1 shows an event tree for one of the treasure scenarios we invented in the last chapter, the one in which you tossed a coin three times and received a treasure if all three tosses did *not* come up heads.

There are three events on this event tree: the first toss, the second toss, and the third toss. Each of these events has been assigned an identifying letter. Toss #1 is event A. Toss #2 is event B. Toss #3 is event C.

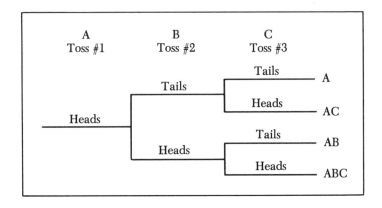

Figure 3.1. Event tree for treasure scenario

These events are identified at the top of the drawing by name and letter, in sequence from left to right. The actual "tree" is directly below this. It is made up of a series of lines that represent the connections between the events. The events themselves are represented by the *branch points,* where one line branches off into two lines, representing the two possible outcomes (heads or tails) of each coin-tossing event. The label on each line tells us whether the outcome was heads or tails. Any complete sequence of events leading from the left-hand side of the tree to the right-hand side is called an *accident sequence.* (A coin that comes up heads can be considered an "accident," because it is definitely not in your best interest.)

At each branch point, the top branch represents a toss of tails and the lower branch a toss of heads. This order is not arbitrary. It is traditional in fashioning an event tree to place the desirable outcome of an event on the top branch and the undesirable outcome on the bottom branch. In this case, a toss of heads is undesirable because three heads mean that you will be shot. A toss of tails is desirable because even one toss of tails means that you will receive the treasure.

You'll notice that one outcome has been ignored in this event tree: the possibility that the first toss will come up tails. That's because an event tree is designed for studying *undesirable* event sequences. If the first coin comes up tails, then there is no way that the sequence can be undesirable, since we know from the very first toss that you are not going to toss three heads in a row. Thus, we ignore the entire half of the event space that begins with this event. The reason for this will become clearer when we show you how event trees are used to describe technological failures.

The letters on the far right-hand side of the event tree represent the "names" of the accident sequences. The name of an accident sequence consists of the letters representing each event in the sequence that takes the lower branch at a branch point—that is, all undesirable events in the sequence. (Because *all* accident sequences begin with an undesirable heads outcome for event A, all of the event sequences on the tree begin with the letter A.) Accident sequence AC, for instance, represents the sequence in which both toss #1 (event A) and toss #3 (event C) come up heads.

Only one of these accident sequences is *totally* undesirable: sequence ABC, the one in which all three tosses come up heads. This is the sequence that will get you shot. We determine the probability of this sequence by multiplying together the probabilities of all the undesirable events in this sequence, which in this case are the probabilities of toss #1, toss #2, and toss #3 coming up heads. Even if we don't know the probabilities off the top of our heads, we can write the multiplication like this:

$$P_A \times P_B \times P_C = P_{ABC}$$

The letter P stands for probability. P_A is the probability of a bad outcome on event A, P_B is the probability of a bad outcome on event B, P_C is the probability of a bad outcome on event C, and P_{ABC} is the probability for this entire accident sequence. As you might recall from the last chapter, the probability of a bad outcome (tossing heads) in each of these events is 50 percent. Thus, we can plug in these figures and perform the actual calculation just as we did in the last chapter:

$$50\% \times 50\% \times 50\% = 12.5\%$$

P_{ABC}—the probability that event ABC will take place—is 12.5 percent.

■ ■ ■

Now let's create an event-tree analysis for a slightly more complicated system, the Morning Wake-up System that we devised in the last chapter. Figure 3.2 shows an event-tree diagram for this system.

The Morning Wake-up System consists of four component systems, each of which has a certain probability of failing on a given morning. These systems, listed along the top of the diagram, are the alarm (A), Mom (B), Al (C), and you (D). The event tree itself shows all accident sequences that would result if the alarm clock failed. Just as in the last tree, when we did not include the sequences that resulted when the first coin came up tails, we do not include

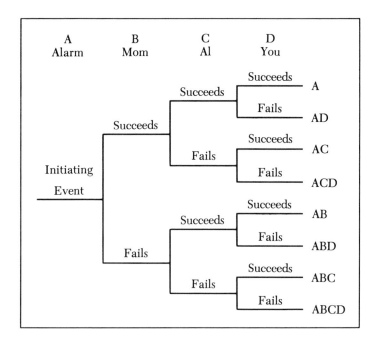

**Figure 3.2. Event tree for
Morning Wake-up System**

here the sequences that result when the alarm clock works properly. The event tree includes only accident sequences, that is, sequences that are initiated by an accident, in this case the failure of the alarm clock. If the alarm clock works successfully, then the backup systems—and their failures and successes—are irrelevant. Thus, we refer to the alarm clock failure as the *initiating event* of the event tree.

In this event tree, and in all of the event trees that follow, the top branch at each branch point represents the successful operation of the system whose name is directly above that branch point, while the lower branch represents the failure of that system. Because branch points in an event tree never have more (or less) than two branches, there is no way to represent partial successes or partial failures. If the alarm clock runs slow and wakes you up a half-hour late, for instance, this might count as a partial failure. On the event tree, however, it would count as an absolute failure. Because partial failures are usually treated in an event tree as absolute failures, the probabilities calculated with the event tree sometimes err on the side of conservatism. That is, the probability of complete failure may look larger than it actually is. It is better, though, to overestimate the probability that a system will fail than to underestimate it.

As in the previous event tree, only one accident sequence—ABCD—leads to total failure of the system. We can calculate this failure with the equation $P_A P_B P_C P_D = P_{ABCD}$. Using the probabilities of failure for each branch point that we assumed in Chapter Two, we get the following:

$$5\% \times 19\% \times 46\% \times 98\% = .428\%$$

The probability of accident sequence ABCD is, therefore, .428 percent.

■ ■ ■

The event tree assumes that all of the events in the accident sequences occur independently of one another, the way that each toss of a coin is independent of any previously tossed coins. In real life, however, this isn't necessarily so. When we construct an event tree for a technological system, we must be careful to watch for *common-cause failures*, that is, failures of subsystems that are triggered by a common cause.

To show you what this means, let's make some changes in your Morning Wake-up System. Suppose that Mom decides she'd rather sleep late, Al moves away to another town, and you develop a permanent case of sleeping sickness that prevents you from waking up without outside help. This removes all of the redundancy from your system, leaving you at the mercy of a single alarm clock with a 5 percent chance of failing in the course of a year. To protect yourself from the dreadful possibility that you will oversleep, you decide to invest in two new alarm clocks to act as backup systems for the main alarm clock. You set the first backup clock to ring five minutes after the main clock and the second backup clock to ring five minutes later.

There are now three component systems in your Morning Wake-up System: the original alarm clock and the two backup alarm clocks. However, there is a crucial difference between the original clock and these two new clocks. Although the original clock was a windup model, the two new clocks are both electric. Thus, without being aware that you were doing it, you have added a fourth subsystem to the Morning Wake-up System: the electrical system of your house. If this fails—and electrical failures are fairly common, as anyone who has had to sit through a blackout waiting for the power to be restored can tell you—the two new alarm clocks will also fail.

Figure 3.3 shows a possible event tree for the new Morning Wake-up System. It is much like the event tree for the last Morning Wake-up System, except that the names of the subsystems have been changed at the top of the chart. Of course, this means that the probability that each of these new subsystems will fail has also changed. Let's assume that each

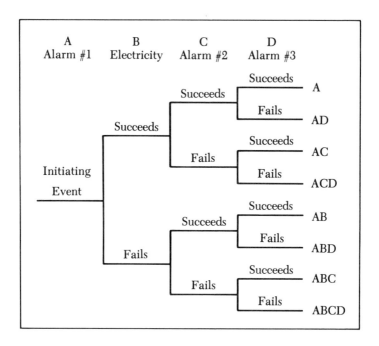

**Figure 3.3. Event tree for
new Morning Wake-up System**

subsystem now has the following probability of failing
on a given morning:

alarm clock 1	5 %
alarm clock 2	1.43%
alarm clock 3	.98%
electricity	6.17%

Once again, only one accident sequence leads to total
system failure—ABCD. The probability of this se-

quence taking place in the course of a year can be calculated as:

$$5\% \times 1.43\% \times .98\% \times 6.17\% = .000043\%$$

Thus the probability that your Morning Wake-up System will fail on a given morning is .000043 percent. Sounds pretty good, doesn't it?

But is it? If you look carefully at the event tree in Figure 3.3, you'll see that some of the accident sequences don't make sense. For instance, sequences AB, ABC, and ABD all assume that the electric power fails, yet one or both of the electric alarm clocks succeed. But that's not possible. If the electric power fails, then *both* of the alarm clocks will fail. An electric alarm clock cannot run without electric power. In this case, the failure of the electric clocks becomes a common-cause failure. Both failures are caused by the failure of a third component system. And that drastically changes the probability of the total system failing. To illustrate these changed probabilities, we have to slice these three nonsensical accident sequences out of the event tree, as shown in Figure 3.4.

In the new event tree, there is only a single accident sequence involving failure of the electric power system. It is called sequence AB, and it inevitably leads to a complete system failure. The probability of sequence AB is simply the probability of event A multiplied by the probability of event B—that is, $P_A \times P_B$—like this:

$$5\% \times 6.17\% = .3085\%$$

Wow! That's quite a change in the probability of a total system failure! Instead of a small probability of .000043

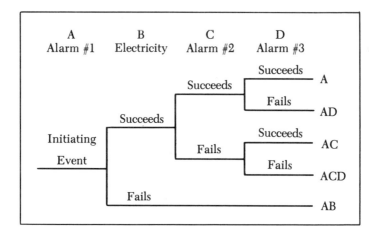

Figure 3.4. Event tree for new Morning Wake-up System, with nonsensical accident sequences removed

percent, we now have a relatively large probability of .3085 percent that the system will fail on a given night, which means we will almost certainly have a wake-up system failure within two school years. Maybe those electric alarm clocks weren't such a good idea after all!

This demonstrates what a difference a common-cause failure can make in an event tree. Because events C and D can be caused by event B, the probability of a total system failure has been greatly increased.

To make matters worse, there is now a second accident sequence in the tree that leads to total system failure: sequence ACD. If both of the electric clocks fail, then it doesn't matter whether the electricity fails or not. After all, clocks can fail for reasons other than power failures. The probability that the system will fail because of accident sequence ACD is $P_A \times P_C \times P_D$, or

$$5\% \times 1.43\% \times .98\% = .0007\%$$

Roughly speaking, we can calculate the total probability of system failure by adding this to the probability of sequence AB, the other sequence that leads to total failure, like this:

$$.3085\% + .0007\% = .3092\%$$

The total probability of system failure is now .3092 percent per morning, which is getting unacceptably high, assuming that you are really intent on not sleeping late.

Is there any way to lower this percentage? Well, you can buy an auxiliary power generator and hook the third clock to it, so that it would keep running even if the main power failed. This would prevent subsystems C and D from being common-cause failures, but it's a pretty expensive way to keep yourself from sleeping late. A better way would be to replace one of the electric clocks with another windup clock or a battery-operated clock so that it would not fail if the main power failed.

There is one element that we have left off our event trees: the human element. If the Morning Wake-up System is to work properly, you must remember to set all of these alarm clocks before you go to bed. If you forget to set them, none of them will ring, and you will probably oversleep. Forgetting to set the alarm clocks, then, makes the failure of all *three* alarm clocks a common-cause failure—even if each clock has a separate power source. If you tend to be an absentminded sort of person, forgetting to set the clocks may be the most important cause of failure in your Morning Wake-up System.

This is true in the real world, as well. As we will see in later chapters, most investigators believe that the human element was the most important factor in the disasters at Three Mile Island, Chernobyl, and Bhopal!

■ ■ ■

Before we move on, there is one more important point that we must make about event trees. In order to calculate the probability of the accident sequences in these event trees, we have used numbers representing the percentage probability that each subsystem will fail. Where did these numbers come from?

In the case of the treasure scenario, the numbers came from logic and experience. Everybody knows that an honest coin has a 50 percent chance of coming up heads after a single toss; that's simply common sense. But how do we know that our windup alarm clock has a 22.1 percent chance of failing? Where did we get this rather precise-sounding number?

The answer, perhaps surprisingly, is that we got it out of thin air. The author of this book made it up. All of the probabilities for failure of the various components of our Morning Wake-up System were made up.

Of course, the Morning Wake-up System itself is fictional and is used here only to illustrate the principles of event-tree construction, so it doesn't really matter that we've used made-up numbers to show how it works. But in the real world we can't go around inventing arbitrary probabilities concerning technological systems that might fail. We must find percentages that reflect the actual probabilities.

As we have said before, these figures are commonly obtained through observation. We study the performance of a system over a period of time and note how often it fails. After enough observation, we have a good idea as to the probability that a given system will fail.

But observation takes time and can even be dangerous. We can't deliberately allow a nuclear reactor to fail or wait to see if it fails just to see if the backup systems work. What if they didn't work? We would be putting too many people at risk. The idea of risk analysis is to predict these failures in advance, so that something can be done about them before they happen.

How, then, are we to estimate the probability that a brand-new piece of technology, whether it be an alarm clock or a nuclear reactor, will fail? Is it even possible to make such an estimate without observing the technology at work over a period of time?

According to some experts, it is possible to estimate the probability that a new technology will fail using yet another kind of diagram, called a *fault tree*, which we will look at in the next chapter.

PREDICTING

FOUR

FAULT TREES

You've bought a new alarm clock to serve as yet another backup system in your Morning Wake-up System. It's a new kind of alarm clock, and you've never owned one quite like it before. You don't know from experience how likely it is to fail. However, you are eager to draw up a new event tree for the Wake-up System, so you visit the manufacturer (Susan B.) of the alarm clock to see if she can tell the probability that your new alarm clock will fail.

Unfortunately, Susan B. tells you that the alarm clock is so new that even she doesn't know how reliable it is. Preliminary tests indicate that it has a pretty low probability of failure, but more advanced tests will need to be conducted before she can give you a more precise figure. Would you be willing to come back in two years?

Seeing how disappointed you are, Susan B. agrees to help you figure out for yourself how reliable the clock is. As it happens, she says, the clock is made from standard alarm clock parts, which have been used in many previous alarm clocks. Although no one knows the failure probability for the entire clock, the failure probability for each of the parts is very well known.

There are three parts in this clock, Susan B. says: the mainspring, the flywheel, and the ratchet gear. She hands you a sheet of paper that gives you the probability that any one of these parts will fail on a given morning:

mainspring .37%

flywheel .03%

ratchet gear .04%

If any *one* of these parts fails, Susan B. says, the entire clock will fail. You stare at the sheet of paper and wonder what good this information does you. The manufacturer smiles and produces a second sheet of paper. On this sheet of paper is a drawing, which we have reproduced in Figure 4.1.

"This is a fault tree," she says, "that shows how the clock can fail."

"Uh, right," you reply, not sure that you see how this drawing tells you anything about the clock you didn't already know. "What are all of these funny boxes?"

"Those are the fault-tree symbols. The rectangle at the top represents the failure of the entire clock. Beneath the rectangle are the things that have to

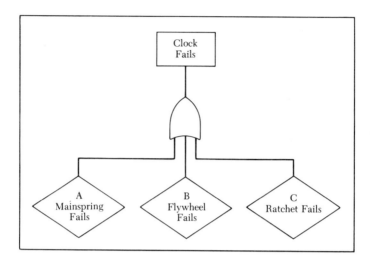

Figure 4.1. Fault tree for alarm clock

happen in order for that failure to take place. For instance, the triangles at the bottom of the chart represent the failure of each of the parts of the clock: the mainspring, the flywheel, and the ratchet gear."

"What about the curved thing in between?"

"That's an OR gate," Susan B. says. "It means that if the mainspring fails OR the flywheel fails OR the ratchet gear fails, it will lead directly to the failure of the entire clock."

"How does this help me figure the probability that the clock will fail?"

"Well," Susan B. says, "we can translate this fault tree into a written equation, like this."

She pulls a piece of paper out of her desk and writes these numbers on it:

$$P_A + P_B + P_C = P_D$$

"The letter P refers to the probability that . . ."

"Yes," you say. "I already know about that. I guess the other letters refer to the letters inside the fault-tree symbols?"

"Exactly," Susan B. says, smiling. "This means that the probability of event D, the failure of the entire clock, is equal to the probability of event A plus the probability of event B plus the probability of event C. All we have to do is add the probabilities together, like this."

The manufacturer writes these numbers underneath the last set of numbers:

$$.37\% + .03\% + .04\% = .44\%$$

"So the probability of the entire clock failing in any given year is .44 percent," she says. "Pretty good, eh?"

"Not bad," you say, "but I was hoping for something even safer. Do you have fault trees like this for any other clocks?"

"As a matter of fact," she says, "we happen to be working on a new clock right now for NASA. They need a superreliable windup alarm clock in case they have a power failure on the space shuttle. This clock is almost identical to the clock you bought, except that it has a double mainspring. If one mainspring fails, it can still run on the second one."

"A *redundant* mainspring!" you say, remembering what you've learned about event trees.

"That's the idea," Susan B. says, pulling another drawing (which we've reproduced in Figure 4.2) from her desk. "Here's the fault tree for the new clock."

"What's this new symbol that looks like an OR gate with a flat bottom?" you ask.

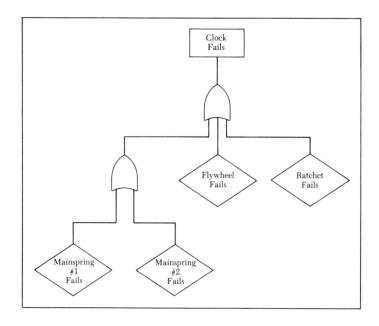

Figure 4.2. Fault tree for NASA alarm clock

"That's an AND gate. It means that mainspring #1 AND mainspring #2 must fail before the clock suffers a mainspring failure. We can calculate the probability of a mainspring failure by multiplying the probability of mainspring #1 failing by the probability of mainspring #2 failing. Since both mainsprings have the same probability of failure, that gives us this equation."

She writes more numbers on the paper:

$$.37\% \times .37\% = .0013\%$$

"The probability of a mainspring failure is now .0013 percent."

"Wow," you say. "That makes the mainspring mechanism a lot safer! But how do we find the probability that the entire clock will fail?"

"We can translate this entire fault tree into this equation," Susan B. says, writing more numbers:

$$(.37\% \times .37\%) + .03\% + .04\% = .07\%$$

"This tells us that we must first multiply together the probabilities that both mainsprings will fail—those are the numbers in parentheses—then add in the probabilities that the flywheel and ratchet will fail. That gives us a probability of .07 percent that the clock will fail on a given morning."

"Now that's a safe clock!" you exclaim. "How much does it cost?"

"Only $400,000," she says. "We're on a government contract."

"Um, that's a little out of my range," you say. "I think I'll stick with the first clock. Anyway, thanks for showing me all about fault trees. Are all fault trees this simple?"

"Oh, no," she says. "Most fault trees are so complicated that we need special computer programs to calculate the probabilities of a system failure." She pulls yet another sheet of paper out of her desk. "Here. This sheet lists most of the symbols that are used in fault trees. You can use it to make fault trees of your own."

"Uh, thanks," you say. The sheet is covered with boxes of different shapes. We've reproduced this sheet for you in Figure 4.3.

"Have fun!" she says and turns back to her work.

■ ■ ■

EVENT REPRESENTATIONS

The rectangle identifies an event that results from the combination of fault events through the input logic gate.

The circle describes a basic fault event that requires no further development. Frequency and mode of failure of items so identified are derived from empirical data.

The triangles are used as transfer symbols. A line from the apex of the triangle indicates a transfer in and a line from the side or bottom denotes a transfer out.

The diamond describes a fault event that is considered basic in a given fault tree. The possible causes of the event are not developed further because the event is of insufficient consequence or the necessary information is unavailable.

The circle within a diamond indicates a subtree exists, but that subtree was evaluated separately and the quantitative results inserted as though a component.

The house is used as a switch to include or eliminate parts of the fault tree as those parts may or may not apply to certain situations.

LOGIC OPERATIONS

AND gate describes the logical operation whereby the coexistance of all input events is required to produce the output event.

OR gate defines the situation whereby the output event will exist if one or more of the input events exists.

or

INHIBIT gates describe a causal relationship between one fault and another. The input event directly produces the output event if the indicated condition is satisfied. The conditional input defines a state of the system that permits the fault sequence to occur, and may be either normal to the system or result from failures.

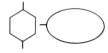

Figure 4.3. Standard fault symbols (from Norman C. Rasmussen *et al., Reactor Safety Study*)

Fault trees were developed at NASA in the 1960s as a method of predicting the failure rates of new and untried space vehicles. At one time, years before the explosion of the space shuttle, NASA's safety record was astounding, considering the complexity and potential risk of the hardware that it developed for the Apollo program. Still, the fault-tree method of analyzing the risk of technological hardware is controversial, and not everyone agrees that it produces accurate descriptions of the probability that a piece of hardware, be it an alarm clock or a space vehicle or a nuclear reactor, will fail.

The idea of the fault tree is that if you take apart an untested piece of hardware, you will find that it is made up of smaller pieces of hardware that have well-known probabilities of failure. By linking together these pieces with AND gates, OR gates, and other kinds of connections, the information can then be translated into equations that can be solved by a computer, to determine the probability that the entire piece of hardware will fail.

Does it work? No one is quite sure. Some of the fault trees created by NASA produced what now seem to be underestimates of hardware failure, and NASA eventually abandoned the use of fault trees in favor of other methods. But fault-tree methodology has improved considerably in the years since the Apollo program, and it is now the preferred method of analyzing hardware risks in the nuclear power industry. Later, we'll see actual fault trees developed for assessing the reliability of the hardware used in this and other industries.

All fault trees are constructed with the failure of the hardware as the topmost event and all paths that lead to that failure shown below it. Any path from an initiating event (usually the failure of some component in the system) to the topmost event is called a *cut set*. The shortest path to the topmost event—that is, the one with the highest probability—is called the *minimal cut set*.

Fault trees are generally used in conjunction with event trees. Once we've analyzed the failure probability of a subsystem using fault-tree analysis, it can then be placed in an event tree with the failure probabilities of other subsystems, many of which have also been calculated using fault trees.

■ ■ ■

Now that we've studied the tools with which we can analyze the risk of complex technological systems, let's look at a complex technological system that has been analyzed using these tools.

PART TWO

NUCLEAR POWER POWER

PREDICTING

FIVE

ENERGY FROM
THE ATOM

A technological society needs energy. In fact, every living thing on earth needs energy, just to live.

Most of the energy on earth comes from the sun, carried across 93 million miles (150 million km) of space in the form of tiny energy packets called photons. It is this energy from the sun, in fact, that creates the phenomenon we know as weather. Differences in air temperature, created by sunlight, make the wind blow, and large differences in temperature cause storms.

Hundreds of millions of years ago, plants developed the ability to trap this energy from the sun and store it in substances called carbohydrates. The plants then use this energy to power the processes that keep them alive.

Animals eat plants to get the energy trapped in these carbohydrate molecules. Other animals then eat

the animals that ate the plants and receive the carbohydrates in turn. The way in which the energy from
the sun passes from plants to animals to still other
animals is called the *food chain*. It is the food chain
that spreads the sun's energy among all living things.
From food, we get the energy that keeps our meta-
bolic processes in motion and enables us to move.

Our machines need energy, too. Surprisingly,
most of the energy that we use to power machines also
comes from the sun. When we pump gasoline into an
automobile, for instance, we are utilizing a fuel made
from the remains of plants and animals that lived and
died millions of years ago. Such fuels are called *fossil
fuels* and are usually found deep beneath the surface
of the earth, where ancient carbohydrates have been
concentrated by great pressures, over long periods of
time. In effect, our automobiles are part of a very old
food chain.

Much—in fact, most—of the energy we use to
power our technology is first put into a form called
electricity. In this form, it can be delivered by wire to
remote locations. There are many ways to convert
existing energy forms (such as the energy of the sun)
into electricity, but only about half a dozen of these
methods are in common use.

One is coal power. Coal is a fossil fuel that can be
burned to generate heat; this heat is used to boil water
to produce steam that turns a turbine that generates
electricity. Like the natural gas used to make gasoline,
coal is made from ancient carbohydrates containing
energy from the sun.

Hydropower uses the energy of flowing water
to turn turbines to produce electricity. Hydropower
generators are usually built inside dams. Since it is
sunlight that evaporates water and moves it uphill to

A coal yard

flow in rivers, hydropower generators also tap the energy of the sun.

Solar power uses the sun's energy more directly. A solar power generator uses solar cells to turn photons from the sun into usable electricity.

The sun contains a huge amount of energy, more than human beings are ever likely to need. Hydropower and solar power are called renewable energy sources, because they tap into this nearly inexhaustible flow of energy. Unfortunately, we have not yet conquered the problems involved in using solar cells for large-scale electricity generation and probably will not do so until well into the next century. Hydropower can be used only in areas where large, swiftly flowing rivers are available and should only be used sparingly because hydropower dams usually harm the environments in which they are built.

Therefore, most of the energy that we use comes from fossil fuels. Fossil fuels have two important drawbacks as a source of energy. One is that they produce air pollution. The other is they are nonrenewable. That is, they will eventually run out.

As our technology becomes more and more complex, our energy demands become greater and greater. Yet our energy resources are limited. How do we resolve this paradox?

Within the next century, we will probably develop new large-scale methods of energy generation, such as nuclear fusion, to take care of the problem (although it wouldn't hurt if we also learned how to build technological systems that demand less energy). In the meantime, especially over the next few decades, there are only two methods of energy generation that can provide us with the large amounts of power that modern technology requires: coal power and nuclear fission.

Nuclear fission, a type of energy that is usually referred to simply as nuclear energy, uses a device called a *reactor* to unleash the energy contained in certain substances found naturally in the earth. Nuclear energy is not a fossil fuel; it does not even use the energy of the sun, as have all of the power sources that we've discussed so far. Neither is nuclear fission a renewable resource, though in theory the supply of nuclear energy on this planet should last for centuries. (In practice, it is running out as quickly as fossil fuels, but it might be possible to build more-efficient nuclear power plants, which will actually produce new fuel while they produce electricity.) Nuclear energy also produces pollution, though by most estimates it is considerably cleaner than fossil fuels such as coal.

From this description, nuclear energy would seem to be the answer to our technological prayers, a source of clean, abundant energy that could last for centuries. But nuclear energy has several unique drawbacks of its own.

In this book, we won't be offering a complete assessment of the pros and cons of nuclear energy. Many books have already been written on this subject. Rather, we are going to discuss the single feature that sets nuclear energy apart most radically from other forms of electricity generation: it is subject to catastrophic failure. It is possible for a nuclear power plant to fail in such a way that, in theory at least, many thousands of people will die. And, in fact, at least one major nuclear catastrophe has already occurred, at Chernobyl in the Soviet Union. We'll be discussing this and other nuclear accidents in Chapter Seven.

*Duquesne Light Nuclear Power Plant
in Shippingsport, Pennsylvania*

First, though, let's take a look at how nuclear power works.

■ ■ ■

In 1905, the great physicist Albert Einstein published a paper in which he proposed that matter and energy were equivalent. That is, matter could, under certain circumstances, change into energy and energy into matter. He even provided an equation, $E = MC^2$, for calculating how much energy a piece of matter is equivalent to. What this equation means is that the energy in a piece of matter is equal to the mass (or weight) of that matter multiplied by the speed of light (a very large number) squared. You don't have to perform this calculation (or even know *how* to perform it) to see that a small amount of matter is equal to a very large amount of energy. If we could tap into the energy bound up in even a relatively small amount of matter, we would have an energy source that could power our technology for a long time to come.

And, in fact, there is a way to tap into at least some of this energy. All matter is made up of tiny particles called *atoms*, and all atoms, in turn, are made up of tinier subatomic particles called *protons*, *electrons*, and *neutrons*. By shuffling the way in which some of these particles are arranged inside the atom, we can turn a tiny amount of the matter in these particles into pure energy. This is the principle behind nuclear weapons—and nuclear reactors.

Perhaps you've seen drawings that purport to represent the structure of atoms (Figure 5.1). The neutrons and protons are bunched together in the center, like a cluster of beach balls, while the tiny electrons orbit in circles around the cluster, like planets about the sun. This is *not* an accurate picture

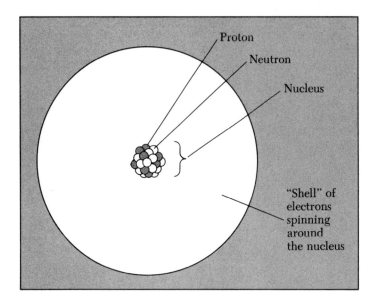

Proton

Neutron

Nucleus

"Shell" of electrons spinning around the nucleus

Figure 5.1. An atom

of how an atom is constructed, but it conveys the essential idea. The electrons orbit around the outer fringes of the atom's structure, forming a kind of hard shell around the atom, while the neutrons and protons cluster together tightly in the center, forming a structure called the *nucleus.*

When atoms link up with other atoms—and atoms are almost always linking up to form larger structures called *molecules*—it is the electron shells that determine how the atoms interact. In scientific jargon, we say that the chemical nature of the atom is determined by the shells of electrons. Different elements—that is, materials made up of different kinds of atoms—behave in a different manner because of the differences in their electron shells. Thus oxygen, to choose but a single example, behaves in a very different way than iron.

The number of electrons surrounding the atom is, in turn, determined by the number of protons in the nucleus. An atom can lose an electron or two without becoming a different kind of atom, but an atom that loses or gains a proton immediately becomes a different kind of atom, that is, an atom of a different element. An atom with a single proton in its nucleus is an atom of hydrogen. An atom with 26 protons is an atom of iron. An atom with 92 protons is an atom of uranium. And so forth. The number of protons in an atom is referred to as the atom's *atomic number*.

The number of neutrons in the atom is determined somewhat more mysteriously. In general, smaller atoms have about the same number of neutrons in their nuclei as protons, while larger atoms have about half again as many neutrons as protons. However, this is by no means invariably true. Hydrogen, for instance, usually has *no* neutrons in its nucleus. The most common type of uranium has 146 neutrons in its nucleus, even though uranium has only 92 protons. Furthermore, most elements exist in several *different* forms, all of which have the same number of protons in their nuclei but different numbers of neutrons. We call these *isotopes* of the element. Isotopes are commonly identified by their *mass number*, which is the total number of protons and neutrons in the nucleus. Thus, the isotope of uranium with 92 protons and 146 neutrons is called uranium-238, or U^{238} for short.

Just as certain structures made of bricks or girders are more stable than others, certain structures of protons and neutrons are more stable than others. And just as a poorly constructed house might fall apart in an attempt to become more stable—a pile of bricks on the ground being more stable than a lopsided house—so a poorly constructed atomic nucleus (an unstable isotope) may rearrange itself to form a more stable atomic nucleus (a stable isotope) and may actually fall apart in the process.

In some cases, a neutron inside the nucleus may turn into a proton, which will convert the atom into an isotope of a completely different element, which may or may not be stable. Certain isotopes of uranium, for instance, can convert spontaneously into isotopes of neptunium, an element with 93 protons in its nucleus. If the new isotopes are also unstable, they may convert into still other elements.

Certain isotopes of the very heavy elements uranium and plutonium, especially uranium-235 (U^{235}) and plutonium-239 (Pu^{239}), can rearrange their nuclei in a very unusual manner. The nuclei of these atoms can actually split apart, so that each atom becomes a pair of much smaller atoms. This process is called *nuclear fission*.

In general, when an unstable nucleus rearranges itself into a more stable nucleus (or nuclei), the resulting nucleus (or nuclei) contains some subatomic particles that it doesn't need. These particles are expelled from the nucleus at high speeds. Usually, these particles are electrons, neutrons, or *alpha particles*. (An alpha particle is identical to the nucleus of a helium atom, consisting of two protons and two neutrons bound tightly together.)

When a large atom, such as an atom of U^{235} or Pu^{239}, fissions into two smaller atoms, a tiny amount of the atom's mass is lost altogether. This lost mass is converted into pure energy, according to Einstein's equation, $E = MC^2$. Usually, this energy takes the form of motion—the rapid motion of a neutron, electron, or alpha particle expelled from the nuclei, for instance. This energy can be harnessed, either in the form of a weapon (the atom bomb) or electricity (the nuclear reactor).

The trick to harnessing the energy of a fissioning atom lies in making a uranium or plutonium atom fission on demand rather than spontaneously. Ordinarily, an atom of uranium or plutonium fissions only when it is good and ready; it might fission today or tomorrow or several thousand years from now. But we can induce an unstable atom to fission by firing a high-speed neutron into its nucleus. If our aim is good, the extra neutron will increase the instability of the atom and cause it to fission immediately.

Of course, if we had to fire a high-speed neutron at every atom in order for it to fission, this would be an awkward and inefficient way of generating energy. Fortunately, a fissioning atom will produce from one to three high-speed neutrons of its own while fissioning, which in turn can collide with the nuclei of other atoms; thus, a single fissioning atom of uranium or plutonium can cause up to three more atoms to undergo fission. And these atoms can, in turn, cause other atoms to fission. This process is called a *chain reaction.*

To produce a chain reaction, we must bring together a certain amount of U^{235} or Pu^{239} atoms. If we bring together too few atoms, or if there are too many atoms of other substances mixed in with the fissionable atoms, the chain reaction will die out as quickly as it has begun, because most of the neutrons will miss the nuclei altogether. (Atomic nuclei are very small, and a neutron must be fired into a large quantity of unstable nuclei for it to have much likeli-

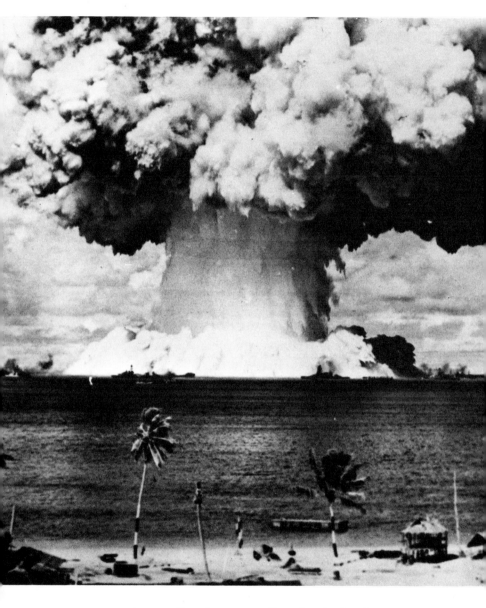

Atomic bomb test on the island of Bikini
in the Pacific Ocean, 1946

hood of hitting one.) The amount of a substance that we must bring together to create a sustained chain reaction is called the *critical mass.*

The only fissionable element that occurs, in any significant amount, in nature is U^{235}. But it occurs in an impure form, mixed in with a considerable amount of U^{238}, which is not fissionable. In fact, only about .7 percent of all uranium is U^{235}. In order to create a critical mass of U^{235}, we must first enrich the uranium, that is, remove as many U^{238} atoms as possible so that a larger percentage of the uranium will be U^{235}.

To make an atomic bomb, uranium is enriched until it is about 90 percent U^{235}. Then, if two less-than-critical masses of enriched uranium are brought together very quickly—usually, by firing the two masses at one another with conventional explosives—the resulting critical mass explodes with tremendous power.

Uranium intended for use in a nuclear power plant is only enriched to about 2 or 3 percent U^{235}. Such poorly enriched uranium cannot explode; thus there is no real danger of a nuclear reactor erupting in a nuclear explosion. But it does generate a lot of heat. Just as coal power uses burning coal to produce steam to power a turbine, nuclear power uses the heat of a critical mass of uranium to produce steam for the same purpose.

Before it is placed in a reactor, the enriched uranium is formed into *fuel pellets,* shaped rather like large vitamin pills or sawed-off bullets, each about 1 inch (2.5 cm) long and .5 inch (1.25 cm) wide. These pellets are in turn placed inside metal tubes called *cladding,* which are then clustered together into *fuel elements.* When enough fuel elements are brought together inside a nuclear reactor to form a critical mass, the resulting chain reaction generates heat. The part of the nuclear reactor where this takes place is called the *reactor core.*

In most U.S. reactors, water is circulated among the fuel elements. The water serves as a *moderator,* which slows down the neutrons produced by fission and makes them more likely to interact with the nuclei of other uranium atoms and sustain the chain reaction. In addition, the water carries the heat of the chain reaction from the reactor core to a separate part of the reactor system, where it is used to generate electricity. Because it carries the heat away from the core, we say that the water is acting as a *coolant.*

Reactors that use ordinary water as a moderator and a coolant are sometimes referred to as *light-water reactors.* (Another type of reactor uses deuterium, or "heavy water," as moderator and coolant. Other types of reactors use elements other than water as a moderator or coolant.) The most common types of light-water reactors are the *boiling-water reactor* (or BWR) and the *pressurized-water reactor* (or PWR). The PWR is the most commonly used reactor in the United States, although about 30 percent of U.S. reactors are BWRS.

Reactor core is lowered into position at a nuclear power plant. Its fuel consists of 14 tons of natural uranium and 165 pounds of enriched uranium. Inset: Scale model of nuclear fuel bundle that consists of 28 pencil bundles of uranium.

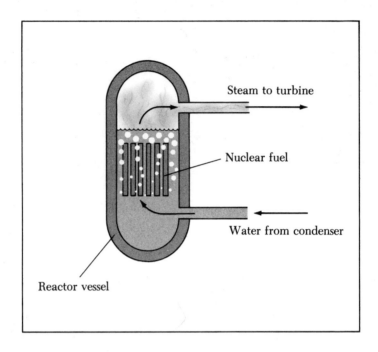

Figure 5.2. Boiling-water reactor. Adapted from
***The New Book of Popular Science,* vol. 2.**

In a boiling-water reactor (see Figure 5.2), the water circulating through the fuel elements is converted directly to steam by the heat of the chain reaction. This steam, in turn, drives the turbine that generates the electricity. When the water cools, it is recirculated through the fuel elements and the process repeats itself. In a pressurized-water reactor (see Figure 5.3), on the other hand, the water that drives the turbine is kept in a separate (but intermingled) set of pipes from the water that circulates through the fuel rods. The heat from the water that circulates through the fuel rods travels through the metal walls of the

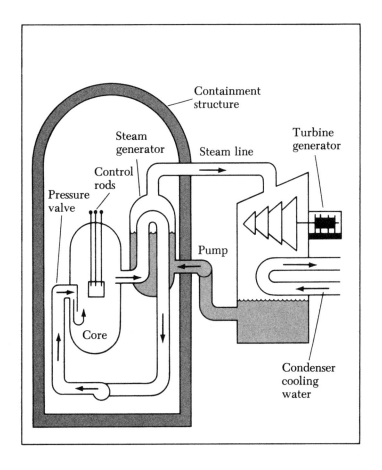

Figure 5.3. Pressurized-water reactor

pipes and heats the water in the second set of pipes, causing it to boil and create steam that drives the turbine. (The name "pressurized-water reactor" refers to the fact that the water that passes through the fuel rods is kept under high pressure, so that it cannot turn into steam.)

To allow the operators of a nuclear reactor to raise or lower the amount of heat produced by the fuel elements, several rods of a neutron-absorbing substance, such as boron, are positioned in such a way that they can be lowered among the fuel elements, where they will absorb the neutrons produced by the atomic fission, thus fine-tuning the intensity of the chain reaction. These are called the *control rods*. In addition, a set of safety control rods is kept suspended above the fuel elements; these will automatically drop into the reactor core in an emergency, halting the chain reaction altogether, a process that is known as *scramming* the reactor.

(The author of this book has heard several stories purporting to explain the origin of the term "scramming." The most likely sounding of these has it that the world's first nuclear reactor, built at the University of Chicago in 1942, had a single safety control rod suspended above it on a rope. Next to the reactor stood a graduate student with an ax, whose job was to cut the rope in case the reactor got out of control. The graduate student was called the safety control rod ax man—or SCRAM, for short.)

Compared to, say, coal power, nuclear power is quite efficient. The amount of uranium required to generate a given amount of electricity is a mere fraction of the amount of coal required to generate the same amount of electricity. (Unfortunately, the amount of uranium available on this planet is only a fraction of the amount of coal, which tends to cancel out this advantage. Nonetheless, there are ways to make nuclear reactors use these limited fuel supplies more efficiently, as we shall see later.) Furthermore, in normal operation nuclear power does not create the severe atmospheric pollution attributable to coal power.

Unfortunately, nuclear power has one important drawback when compared to coal power: the nuclear fuel, and some of its by-products, are *radioactive.*

We saw earlier that unstable atomic nuclei often expel unwanted particles, such as electrons, neutrons, and alpha particles, at high speeds. Although these particles are much too small to be seen, even with the most powerful microscopes available, they can damage the atoms and molecules in the tissues of any living organisms, such as human beings or other animals, that happen to be nearby. This bombardment of submicroscopic particles is called *radiation.* A substance that produces radiation is said to be radioactive.

(Radiation made up of tiny particles is called *ionizing radiation,* because it can rip apart molecules and atoms to form electrically charged particles called *ions.* Some radioactive substances also produce a second kind of radiation called the *gamma ray,* which is a form of electromagnetic radiation similar to an X ray. Like ionizing radiation, gamma rays can also be deadly to living tissue.)

A human being (or other animal) exposed to a large amount of radiation will die of radiation sickness, the result of massive tissue damage. A human being exposed to a smaller amount of radiation will not die of radiation sickness but may suffer from a more subtle form of tissue damage that could result in cancer years or decades after the exposure.

How much radiation is a "large amount"? To answer that question, we first must have a yardstick with which to measure radiation exposure. Unfortunately, different kinds of radiation are measured using different yardsticks. The *roentgen,* for instance, is used to measure certain kinds of radiation. More useful to us here, however, is the *rem,* or *roentgen-equivalent man,* a measure of the amount of radiation actually absorbed into the body of someone exposed to one roentgen of radiation. Because exposures of one rem or greater are fairly rare, it is common to measure radiation exposure with the *millirem* (*mrem*), or 1/1000th of a rem.

An exposure of 1,000 rems or more will invariably lead to death by radiation sickness; an exposure of 500 rems has about a 50 percent chance of resulting in death by radiation sickness. Exposures of less than 50 rems never produce radiation sickness but may result in death by cancer later. (Larger exposures, if they are not immediately fatal, may also result in cancer later.)

There is no such thing as a "safe" exposure to radiation. Even exposure to a single particle of radiation can result in cancer, though physicist Bernard L. Cohen, an outspoken proponent of nuclear power, estimates that the chance that a single particle of radiation will cause cancer is roughly one in 50 quadrillion (50,000,000,000,000,000,). The risk from small exposures to radiation is a subject of some controversy, but most scientists agree that it is slight.

Radioactive materials are sometimes released from nuclear power plants, resulting in an exposure of several millirems to each person in the population of the surrounding area. This increases the chance that members of this population will eventually develop cancer, but only by a very small amount. To put the matter into perspective, each of us is exposed every day to radiation from natural sources. Some of this radiation comes from *cosmic rays,* high-speed particles from space, launched toward earth by the energy of exploding stars or collapsing black holes many light-years away. Some of it is in the form of radioactive building materials in our houses and apartments, which release a radioactive gas called *radon*. (Ironically, houses that are heavily insulated to conserve heat—and therefore reduce the need for electrical power—often build up large amounts of radon gas, exposing their occupants to as much as several rems per year.) And some of it is from naturally radioactive substances in our food, which actually become parts of our body tissue when we eat them. Thus, our own flesh is slightly radioactive.

Collectively, we refer to the radiation from these various sources as natural background radiation. This background radiation is not new; it has been around for billions of years. Our distant ancestors were exposed to it, long before nuclear power plants existed.

Altogether, the average American receives about 100 mrems of natural background radiation every year, or about 1 mrem every three or four days. This amount varies according to where a person lives, however. Residents of Denver, Colorado, for instance, receive about 200 mrems of radiation every year, because their city is situated high above sea level (and therefore has less atmosphere above it to shield out cosmic rays) and because the soil in the American West is rich in radioactive elements. Proponents of nuclear power are fond of pointing out that a person who moves to Denver to get away from a nuclear power plant will actually receive more excess radiation in Denver than he or she is ever likely to receive from a nuclear reactor.

Does this mean that residents of Denver are more likely to develop cancer than, say, residents of Washington, D.C.? No. Surprisingly, Denver residents are *less* likely to develop cancer, because the air that they breathe is relatively free of other types of pollution. Only a small percentage—probably less than 1 percent —of all cancers are caused by radiation. Thus, the residents of Denver may be more likely to develop cancer from exposure to background radiation, but this barely affects the overall likelihood that they will develop cancer and is more than compensated for by the reduction in other cancer-causing influences, such as air pollution. A person who smokes has a vastly greater chance of developing cancer from cigarette smoke than a person who lives near a nuclear plant has of developing cancer from radiation.

Still, there is a small but frightening possibility that a nuclear power plant may release an unusually large amount of radioactive material, perhaps sufficient to expose members of the nearby population to hundreds or even thousands of rems of radiation— i.e., enough radiation to produce radiation sickness in a small portion of the population and eventual cancers in a much larger portion. The only kind of accident that is likely to result in such a release of radioactive materials is the so-called *meltdown*. Probably, the cause of such a meltdown would be a *loss-of-coolant accident*, or LOCA.

LOCA is the overall term used by the nuclear power industry to describe a failure to supply the reactor core with water or any other substance used as a coolant. Without a coolant, heat will continue to build up in the fuel elements until they actually melt. Even if the control rods are dropped into the core to turn off the chain reaction, the so-called daughter elements—the radioactive by-products of the fission reaction—will continue to produce roughly 7 percent as much heat as the uranium fuel elements, enough to melt right through the floor of the reactor building. This is sometimes referred to as *the China syndrome*, in the mistaken (or humorous) belief that the melting reactor will burrow right through the planet Earth and come out on the other side. In fact, it will probably descend about 20 feet (6 m) before coming to rest in a glass cauldron created when its own tremendous heat fuses the surrounding sand and dirt.

Most nuclear reactors in the United States are surrounded by containment buildings, concrete structures designed to withstand earthquakes, hurricanes, even airplane crashes. But no containment building could withstand the heat of a melting reactor. And once the reactor has melted its way through the containment building floor, it can release radioactive materials into the groundwater, where it will find its way into the surrounding environment, eventually returning to the surface and exposing members of the nearby population.

Worse still, it is possible for certain elements that might form during a meltdown, such as hydrogen, to produce a non-nuclear explosion that could crack the containment building, propelling radioactive materials directly into the atmosphere. If weather conditions are right, these radioactive materials could spread for great distances around the reactor, exposing hundreds, thousands, or—in a worst-case scenario—tens or hundreds of thousands of people to dangerous levels of radiation. Such a meltdown would be a catastrophe indeed.

To guard against such a catastrophe, a typical reactor contains a number of emergency systems. For instance, the *emergency core-cooling system*, or ECCS, provides a backup coolant system in case the main coolant system fails. In fact, most systems in a nuclear

power plant have one or more backup systems, greatly increasing the redundancy of the overall nuclear reactor system. As we saw in Part One of this book, this redundancy reduces the probability that the entire system will fail.

A meltdown is a scary possibility. It is tempting to suggest—and, indeed, it has been suggested on numerous occasions—that we should abandon nuclear power altogether, simply because such a thing as a meltdown is possible.

But possible isn't the same thing as probable. It is fair to ask what the probability of such a meltdown might be, so that we can assess the risk of nuclear power in comparison to the risk of, say, coal power. Coal, while it is not subject to such catastrophic accidents as a meltdown, is nonetheless a risky technology. According to some estimates, as many as 50,000 people die *every* year because of coal power— from coal-related air pollution, accidents in coal mines, and so forth.

Has any one attempted to assess the risks of nuclear power using the techniques of probabilistic risk analysis (or PRA)? Yes. In fact, as we suggested

Workers inside
a nuclear reactor
containment building
wear protective gear
to perform maintenance
operations during a
temporary plant shutdown.

earlier, PRA techniques have probably been used more extensively on nuclear power than on any other risky technology.

In the next chapter, we'll look at past attempts to assess the risk of nuclear power. And, in Chapter Seven, we'll look at some nuclear accidents and see how well they fit the risk patterns that the risk assessors have predicted.

PREDICTING

SIX

ASSESSING THE NUCLEAR RISK

In 1956 and 1957, even as the first working nuclear power plants were being built, the U.S. government was studying the risk of reactor failure. At the time, such risk assessments were the responsibility of the Atomic Energy Commission (AEC). In 1957, the commission released its first study on the dangers of nuclear power, government document WASH-740, entitled *Theoretical Consequences of Major Accidents in Large Nuclear Power Plants.* It described a possible reactor accident and concluded that it might result in as many as 3,400 deaths, 43,000 injuries, and $7 billion worth of damage.

WASH-740, as it is commonly known, was a deterministic study. That is, it did not attempt to assess the probability of such an accident but merely described the way in which it might happen. Nonetheless, the accident described in the report was quite frightening, and the AEC hoped that future research might prove that WASH-740 was unduly pessimistic. But when an updated version of the report was produced in 1964, it was decided that in fact the earlier report had *underestimated* the possible severity of a nuclear-reactor accident. The updated report suggested that as many as 45,000 fatalities might be possible in a worst-case accident.

In the 1970s, increasing public fears about the dangers of nuclear power put pressure on the AEC to produce a more detailed study of reactor safety, one that would cite actual probabilities of various reactor accidents so that the risk of nuclear power could be accurately assessed once and for all. In 1972, an independent team of investigators was assembled under the direction of Dr. Norman C. Rasmussen, a physicist from the Massachusetts Institute of Technology. In 1975, the Rasmussen team—now under the supervision of the AEC's successor, the Nuclear Regulatory Commission (NRC)—produced government document WASH-1400, the *Reactor Safety Study*, commonly known as the Rasmussen report.

The Rasmussen report is a monumental document, in more ways than one. More than 2,000 pages long, it was the first detailed attempt to apply the methods of probabilistic risk analysis to a technology as complex as nuclear power. Packed to the brim with event trees and fault trees exploring most aspects of reactor operation, the report cited specific probabilities for all types of reactor accidents. The report sums up its findings like this:

The principal effort in this study has been devoted to accidents in which core melting could potentially occur and to the consequences of such accidents. The insights gained from this effort are as follows:

■ *The work in this study has shown that melting of the reactor core does not necessarily result in an accident having large public consequences. Indeed, in the unlikely event that a core were to melt, there is a spectrum of possible accidents that can occur.*

■ *For the most likely course of events following the melting of a core, the number of fatalities expected is much smaller than those that commonly occur in accidents such as fires, explosions, and crashes of a commercial jet airplane. In addition, the likelihood of a core melt is calculated to be much smaller than any of the above.*

■ *Previous analyses of the consequences of reactor accidents have generally emphasized those that could occur under conditions of poor atmospheric dispersion and in locations involving relatively high population densities. In actuality, there are wide varieties of weather conditions and population densities where reactors are located. When appropriate frequencies of occurrence are assigned to weather conditions and population densities, these can cause potential accident consequences to increase by 100 to 1,000 times; however, the probability of such accidents could decrease by generally similar factors.*[4]

In a series of questions and answers, the Executive Summary of the report cites the actual risk of various reactor accidents. "From the viewpoint of a person living in the general vicinity of a reactor," according to the report, "the likelihood of being killed in any one year in a reactor accident is one chance in 5 billion, and the likelihood of being injured in any one year in a reactor accident is one chance in 75,000,000."[5]

"How likely is a core melt accident?" the report asks, then answers: "The Reactor Safety Study carefully examined the various paths leading to core melt. Using methods developed in recent years for estimating the likelihood of such accidents, a probability of occurrence was determined for each core melt accident identified. These probabilities were combined to obtain the total probability of melting the core. The value obtained was about one in 20,000 per reactor per year. With 100 reactors operating, as is anticipated for the U.S. by about 1980, this means that the chance for one such accident is one in 200 per year."[6]

The most likely effects of a core melt accident are described in the chart in Figure 6.1, taken from the report. The average annual risk from nuclear accidents compared to other risks is shown in Figure 6.2, also from the report. As for the question, "What is the number of fatalities and injuries expected as a result of a core melt accident?" the report answers it this way:

A core melt accident is similar to many other types of major accidents such as fires, explosions, dam failures, etc., in that a wide range of consequences is possible depending on the exact conditions under which the accident occurs. In the case of core melt, the consequences would depend mainly on three factors: the amount of radioactivity released, the way it is dispersed by the prevailing weather conditions, and the number of people exposed to the radiation. With these three factors known, it is possible to make a reasonable estimate of the consequences.

	Consequences
Fatalities	< 1
Injuries	< 1
Latent fatalities per year	< 1
Thyroid nodules per year	< 1
Genetic defects per year	< 1
Property damage[a]	< 1,000,000

[a]This does not include damage that might occur to the plant or costs for replacing the power generation lost by such damage.

Figure 6.1. Most likely consequences of a core melt accident

Type of Event	Probability of 100 or More Fatalities	Probability of 1000 or More Fatalities
Man–caused		
Airplane crash	1 in 2 years	1 in 2000 years
Fire	1 in 7 years	1 in 200 years
Explosion	1 in 16 years	1 in 120 years
Toxic gas	1 in 100 years	1 in 1000 years
Natural		
Tornado	1 in 5 years	very small
Hurricane	1 in 5 years	1 in 25 years
Earthquake	1 in 20 years	1 in 50 years
Meteorite impact	1 in 100,000 years	1 in 1,000,000 years
Reactors		
100 plants	1 in 100,000 years	1 in 1,000,000 years

Figure 6.2. Average probabilities of major man-caused and natural events

The study calculated the health effects and the probability of occurrence for 140,000 possible combinations of radioactive release magnitude, weather type, and population exposed. The probability of a given release was determined from a careful examination of the probability of various reactor system failures. The probability of various weather conditions was obtained from weather data collected at many reactor sites. The probability of various numbers of people being exposed was obtained from U.S. census data for current and planned U.S. reactor sites. These thousands of computations were carried out with the aid of a large digital computer.

The results showed that the probability of an accident resulting in 10 or more fatalities is predicted to be about 1 in 3,000,000 per plant per year. The probability of 100 or more fatalities is predicted to be about 1 in 10,000,000 and for 1,000 or more, 1 in 100,000,000. The largest value reported in the study was 3,300 fatalities, with a probability of about one in a billion. . . .

If a group of 100 similar plants are considered, then the chance of an accident causing 10 or more fatalities is 1 in 30,000 per year. For accidents involving 1,000 or more fatalities the number is 1 in 1,000,000 per year. Interesting, this value coincides with the probability that a meteor would strike a U.S. population center and cause 1,000 fatalities.[7]

The bulk of the report consists of a detailed description of the methods used to reach these conclusions. It states:

Methodologies developed over the past 10 years by the Department of Defense and the National Aeronautics and Space Administration were used in the study. As used in this study, these techniques, called event trees and fault trees, helped to define potential accident paths and their likelihood of occurrence.

An event tree defines an initial failure within the plant. It then examines the course of events which follow as determined by the operation or failure of various systems that are provided to prevent the core from melting and to prevent the release of radioactivity to the environment. Event trees were used in this study to define thousands of potential accident paths which were examined to determine their likelihood of occurrence and the amount of radioactivity that they might release.

Fault trees were used to determine the likelihood of failure of the various systems identified in the event tree accident paths. A fault tree starts with the definition of an undesired event, such as the failure of a system to operate, and it determines, using engineering and mathematical logic, the ways in which the system can fail. Using data covering 1) the failure of components such as pumps, pipes, and valves, 2) the likelihood of operator errors, and 3) the likelihood of maintenance errors, it is possible to estimate the likelihood of system failure, even where no data on total system failure exist.[8]

Hundreds of pages in the report are devoted to the actual event trees and fault trees used in calculating accident probabilities, including detailed descriptions of how they were created. A pair of simplified event trees for a large loss-of-coolant accident (LOCA), used as an example in the *Reactor Safety Study*, is shown in Figure 6.3.[9] These sample event trees (which were, as the report says, "greatly simplified for illustrative

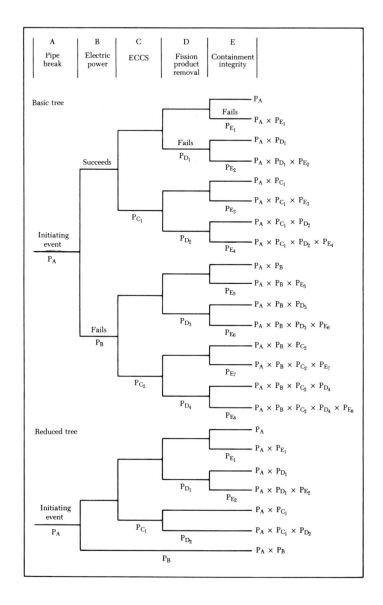

Figure 6.3. Simplified event trees for a large loss-of-coolant accident (LOCA). Adapted from Norman C. Rasmussen *et al.*, *Reactor Safety Study*.

purposes") assume that a LOCA could occur as the result of five events: (1) a pipe break, (2) failure of electric power, (3) failure of the emergency core-cooling system (ECCS), (4) failure of fission-product removal, and (5) failure of the containment building.

These event trees were constructed using the rules discussed in Chapter Three. The upper branch at each branch point represents the successful operation of the system shown at the top of the chart; the lower branch represents the failure of that system. The first event, which does not branch, is the initiating event. Only in the event of a pipe break (the initiating event) followed by the failure of systems C (the ECCS), D (the fission-product removal), and E (the containment building) would an actual release of radioactive substances take place.

However, because a failure of the electric power system can cause all of these systems to fail in a common-cause failure, two versions of the event tree are shown here. The first contains several nonsensical accident sequences in which the power fails but systems such as the ECCS, which could not function without power, operate successfully. The second event tree, shown underneath the first, eliminates these accident sequences, greatly simplifying the event tree. Now two accident sequences, AB and ACDE, all lead to a total system failure. The probability of these sequences can be calculated with the equations that we showed you in Chapter Three, $P_A \times P_B = P_{AB}$ and $P_A \times P_C \times P_D = P_{ACD}$. The total probability of a total system failure—and, therefore, a release of radioactive substances to the environment—is the sum of P_{AB} and P_{ABC}.

The actual probability of these failures taking place was calculated with the aid of fault trees, as discussed in Chapter Four. A sample fault tree from the Rasmussen report—a portion of a larger fault tree used to calculate the probability of a failure in the electric power system of a nuclear reactor—is shown in Figure 6.4.[10] This simplified fault tree assumes that there are two immediate causes for a power failure, the failure of the AC power supply to the engineered safety features (ESF), such as the ECCS, and the failure of the DC power supply to the ESF. (Each of these, presumably, is supplied from a separate source, so that they are unlikely to represent a common-cause failure.) Loss of AC power, in turn, is caused by the simultaneous loss of on-site AC power to ESFs (i.e., a failure of a generator located at the power plant) or loss of off-site power to ESFs (i.e., the failure of a second, remote generator used as backup for the on-site generator). The curlicue symbols at the end of several lines in this fault tree indicate that these events are in turn the result of other events, not shown on this partial chart.

Obviously, the event tree in Figure 6.3 represents only one of many possible paths to a loss-of-coolant accident. And, indeed, the report contains many event trees for a wide variety of initiating events. Similarly, the fault tree in Figure 6.4 represents only one of many different subsystems that were analyzed by the Rasmussen team.

Figure 6.5[11] shows an event tree that actually was used by the Rasmussen team to calculate the probability of a certain kind of small LOCA. It's not necessary to understand all of the events in this tree to appreciate the complexity of it. Similarly, the fault tree in Figure 6.6[12] is one of several used by the Rasmussen team to calculate the probability of failure of a spray-injection emergency cooling system used in PWR reactors. Using the chart of fault-tree symbols in Figure 4.3, you should be able to work out the flow of events in this chart, though the designation of the individual events is somewhat cryptic.

As the report points out, it is not enough to simply calculate the probability that radioactive materials will be released into the atmosphere. It is also necessary to calculate the spread of these materials and their effect on the population surrounding the plant. To calculate the way in which the radioactive materials would spread, the Rasmussen team used a mathematical model known as a Gaussian plume to represent weather conditions. As the report states, "[t]he Gaussian plume model characterizes weather in six stability classes, A through F. Weather type A is unstable and type F is very stable. Wind speed is also characterized by parameters that give the spreading rate in the horizontal and vertical directions."[13] In short, a great deal of complicated mathematics is used to calculate the way in which radioactive materials would spread under a variety of weather conditions.

Did the Rasmussen report, which characterized a major nuclear accident as having roughly the same probability as a meteor strike on a large city (which has never happened), allay public fears about nuclear power? Far from it. The report has been controversial ever since its publication in 1975. In fact, it was controversial even before its publication, when draft copies of the results were made available, and remains so to this day. Groups critical of the nuclear power industry, and even some groups sympathetic to the industry, have found a number of faults in the report, many of which have been proven valid by subsequent events.

A major critique of the Rasmussen report was

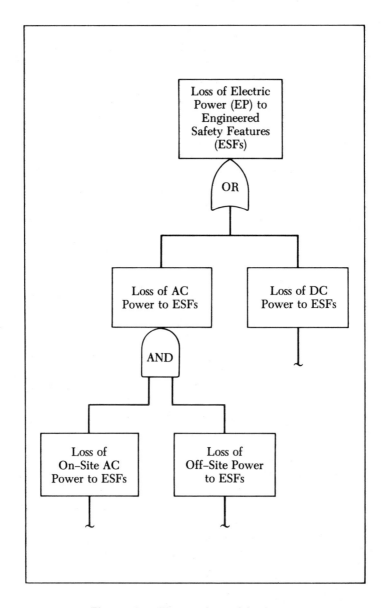

Figure 6.4. Illustration of fault tree development. Adapted from Norman C. Rasmussen et al., *Reactor Safety Study.*

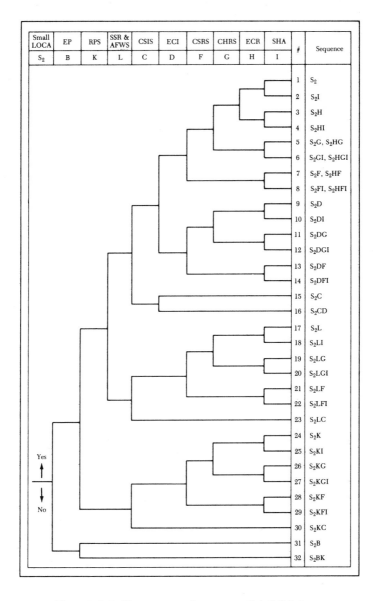

Figure 6.5. Event tree for a small LOCA in a
pressurized-water reactor. Adapted from
Norman C. Rasmussen *et al., Reactor Safety Study.*

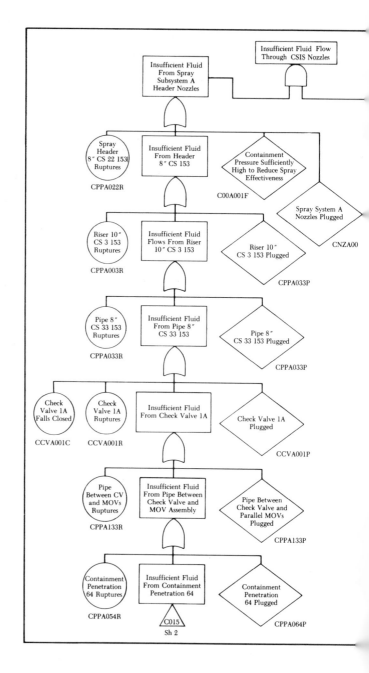

**Figure 6.6. Detailed fault tree of
pressurized-water reactor containment spray-**

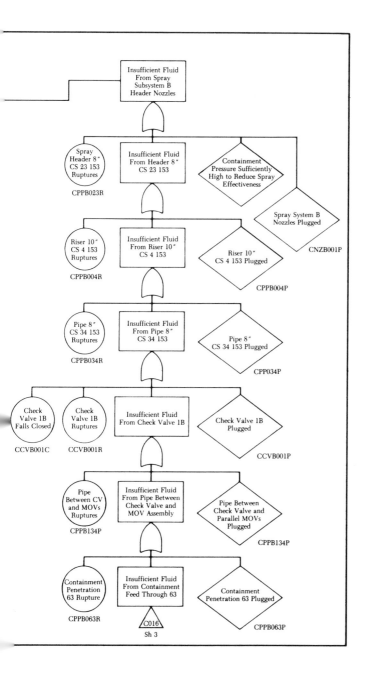

injection system. Adapted from Norman C. Rasmussen *et al., Reactor Safety Study.*

published in 1977 by the Union of Concerned Scientists (UCS), an organization formed in the early 1970s to oppose the proliferation of both nuclear weapons and nuclear reactors. The critique, entitled *The Risks of Nuclear Power Reactors: A Review of the NRC Reactor Safety Study WASH-1400*, is in large part a criticism of probabilistic risk assessment itself. According to the UCS,

The methodology is in principle a powerful one but in practical application, in the aerospace industry and especially in the nuclear area, it has important deficiencies. While useful for comparative risk studies, it is incapable of providing absolute values of probabilities. The obstacles to providing these probabilities for nuclear plants include:

- *an inability to guarantee that all important accident sequences have in fact been identified,*

- *a data base on component reliability that is incomplete and uncertain,*

- *the impossibility of identifying and assessing properly all of the consequences of design errors,*

- *the difficulties in treating common-cause failure modes in a fully satisfactory manner,*

- *the uncertain role of human error, an intractable and capricious element in risk analysis, and*

- *the risk of sabotage.*[14]

In the UCS critique and elsewhere, the two major criticisms of the Rasmussen report concern common-cause failures and human error. Although the Rasmussen team went to considerable lengths to take both into account, subsequent experience has shown that the report may have seriously underestimated the effect that these two factors have on the probability of catastrophic reactor failures.

It is the view of the UCS, and of other groups opposed to nuclear power, that the Rasmussen report, far from being an independent and unbiased view of the perils of nuclear power (as originally billed by the AEC), is in fact an attempt by the nuclear power industry to "paper over" the problem of catastrophic reactor failure. Among groups opposed to nuclear power, WASH-1400 is commonly referred to as "Whitewash 1400."

When the Rasmussen report was published in 1975, a catastrophic reactor failure was still only a theoretical possibility. Despite nearly two decades of nuclear power, a core meltdown had never occurred. In the intervening years, however, there have been two major nuclear accidents, a partial core meltdown at the Three Mile Island Nuclear Energy Plant Unit 2 in Pennsylvania and the total meltdown of the nuclear reactor at Chernobyl in the Soviet Union. What light have these accidents cast on the probabilistic risk analysis performed by the Rasmussen team? We'll look at these accidents, and their implications for probabilistic risk analysis, in the next chapter.

PREDICTING

SEVEN

FROM
THREE MILE ISLAND
TO CHERNOBYL

The Unit 2 nuclear reactor on Three Mile Island near Harrisburg, Pennsylvania—TMI-2, as we shall call it —is a pressurized-water reactor, or PWR for short. As you'll recall from the description in Chapter Five, a PWR maintains two separate water systems, which we'll refer to as the *primary system* and the *secondary system*. The primary system circulates pressurized water through the fuel elements to carry heat out of the reactor core. The secondary system, the pipes of which are closely interlaced with those in the primary system, receives the heat from the primary system and uses it to boil water, which is circulated through a turbine and used to generate electric power.

At 4:00 A.M. on the morning of March 28, 1979, the pump that circulated water in the secondary system at TMI-2 stopped working. Within seconds, the flow of water inside the secondary system had ceased.

*Aerial view of the Three Mile Island
nuclear power plant in Harrisburg, Pennsylvania,
site of a serious nuclear accident in 1979.*

Without the water in the secondary system to carry heat away from the primary system, the temperature of the water in the primary system began to go up, and with it, the water pressure. When the water pressure in the primary system exceeded a certain level— roughly 2,255 pounds per square inch—a relief valve (called the PORV, or pilot-operated relief valve) opened to release some of the water from the system, allowing it to drain into an emergency tank. Eight seconds later, however, with the pressure in the primary system still rising, the safety control rods automatically dropped into place among the fuel elements, scramming the reactor.

At this point, roughly ten seconds after the initial failure, the fission reaction that normally generated heat within the reactor core at TMI-2 ceased. But the reactor core continued to generate heat. Radioactive elements created by earlier fission processes simmered within the core, releasing about 6 percent as much heat as uranium fission. To cool the core, three emergency water pumps turned on. But the water from two of them never arrived at its destination. A pair of valves had accidentally been left closed a few days earlier, during routine maintenance, and they now blocked the circulation of the emergency cooling water. To make matters worse, the PORV valve that had opened in the primary system to remove water pressure failed to close. Water continued draining from the primary system, and the tank into which it drained filled quickly to overflowing. Radioactive water spilled onto the floor of the containment building.

The operators of the TMI-2 reactor, two of whom were in the nearby reactor control room, were quite aware that something was wrong. Alarms sounded throughout the building. A control panel full of emer-

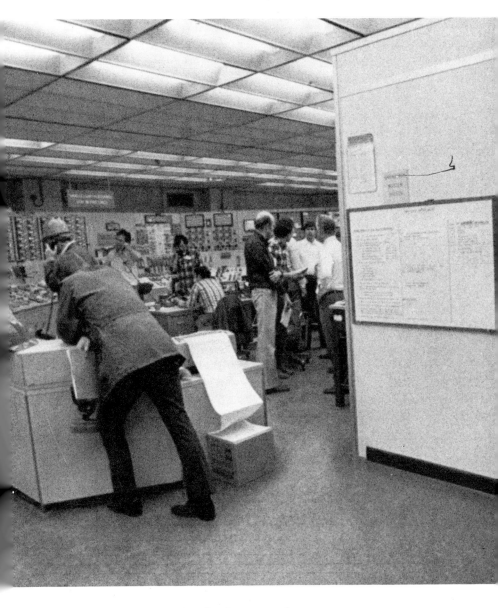

*Inside the control room
at Three Mile Island*

gency lights, signaling malfunctions in the various reactor systems, was flashing wildly; in fact, more than a hundred such lights had been activated during the first seconds of the accident. So confusing was this welter of lights that it may actually have hindered the operators in finding the source of the malfunction. "I would have liked to have thrown away the alarm panel," said one of the operators later. "It wasn't giving us any useful information."[15]

Two of the lights on the panel, however, were reporting a *very* useful piece of information—that the valves on the emergency pumps were closed and their water was not reaching the core. Had the operators known this, they could have opened the valves by hand; at the very least, it would have changed the later course of events. But one of the two emergency lights was covered by a maintenance tag and the other was somehow overlooked. Furthermore, the operators were unaware that the PORV valve had failed to close.

This led to the single biggest error that the operators of the reactor made in dealing with the accident. A little more than an hour after the accident began, one of the operators turned off the only emergency pump that was feeding water to the reactor, in the mistaken belief that the reactor core was receiving a more than adequate supply of water and that it was retaining the water it had already received. Immediately, the level of water surrounding the reactor core began to drop. If nothing were done either to close the valve that was allowing the water to escape from the core or to open the valves that were preventing additional water from reaching the core, the inevitable result would be a meltdown, the first in the history of nuclear power. Radioactive materials would leak from the containment building into the groundwater, and from there to the water supply of the surrounding Pennsylvania community.

A major LOCA—loss-of-coolant accident—was in progress. The reactor core was well on its way to becoming uncovered, probably the worst single thing that can happen to a reactor short of the meltdown itself.

And yet no one was aware that it was happening. The operators believed that the core was adequately covered with water. If the actual nature of the emergency had been understood, almost certainly the operators could have corrected the condition immediately. But by the time the operators became aware that the core had been uncovered, it was almost too late.

In the hours after the accident began, more staff members arrived at the plant. By 7:00 A.M., a site emergency had been proclaimed, meaning that there was a threat of radioactivity being released into the environment. The Nuclear Regulatory Commission was informed at 7:45 A.M. The NRC, in turn, informed the White House at 9:15 A.M.

Unfortunately, no attempt was made to inform the citizens of the area where the accident had occurred. Reporters, suspicious of the activity surrounding the plant, were told that there was a problem with the water pumps, but not what the problem was. Gradually, though, the story trickled out to news media, and a garbled version of the events was made public. By that afternoon, representatives of the wire services, major newspapers, and television networks had arrived in Harrisburg to cover the story. Walter Cronkite, anchorman for the CBS Evening News, opened his nightly report with the words: "It was the first step in a nuclear nightmare; as far as we know at this hour, no worse than that. But a government official said that a breakdown in an atomic power plant in Pennsylvania today is probably the worst nuclear accident to date. . . ."[16] By early evening, local officials were discussing the possibility of evacuating the area around the plant. Eventually, it was decided to evacuate pregnant women and children, those who stood the greatest personal risk from the effects of radiation, from the area.

At TMI-2, meanwhile, the plant operators were desperately trying to fix whatever was wrong with the reactor. It had gradually become obvious that the reactor was not receiving enough water to keep it cool. Two-and-a-half hours after the accident began, the PORV valve that was allowing water to escape the reactor core was finally closed. But another hour passed until more water was injected into the core. And apparently the core remained at least partially uncovered until about 10:30 A.M. By this time, however, the core was so hot that the water was insufficient to cool it off. The effort to bring the reactor to a "cold shutdown"—the point at which heat is no longer generated in the core—continued for several days. The effort to clean up the reactor, to remove the radioactive materials trapped in the containment building, continued for some years after the accident.

■ ■ ■

A full meltdown did not take place at TMI-2, though there was substantial damage to the fuel in the reactor core. A small amount of radiation was released from the containment building during the accident, amounting to somewhat less than 5 mrems additional dosage to individuals in the vicinity of the plant. This is about how much the average person receives from natural background radiation in two and a half weeks.

Was the accident at Three Mile Island a "disaster"? That depends on whom you ask. Opponents of nuclear power argue that the accident at TMI-2 was a "near disaster," a taste of much worse disasters to come if we continue to use nuclear reactors as a source of energy. Supporters of nuclear power, on the other hand, argue that TMI-2 proved just how unlikely a reactor meltdown actually is, since just about everything went wrong during the accident and the reactor core still did not melt, even though earlier calculations had shown that a core left uncovered for such a length of time *should* melt.

Perhaps more to the point, what does the accident at TMI-2 tell us about the probability of future disasters? Does it fall into the range of accidents predicted by the Rasmussen report? Once again, that depends on whom you ask.

Norman Rasmussen himself believes that the report was vindicated by the TMI-2 accident. Writes Rasmussen, "In the hectic days that followed the Three Mile Island accident, it was noted that WASH-1400 contains an accident sequence in which the relief valve on the primary coolant system opened on high system pressure, but failed to close when pressure was reduced. This is exactly what happened during the Three Mile Island accident and was the component failure that led to the accident."[17]

But others point out that the events at TMI-2 were more complex than anything predicted by WASH-1400. In particular, the human element in the Three Mile Island accident proved far more important than the Rasmussen report predicted. It has been pointed out, with some justification, that the TMI reactor would have fared much better than it did if the reactor operators had simply gone out to lunch when the accident began. Although the automatic systems on the reactor worked improperly, they probably would have worked well enough to keep the reactor core covered with water until further investigation had pinpointed the cause and suggested a cure for the problem. But once the operators turned off the emergency pump in the second hour of the accident, TMI became a major LOCA. In a sense, the events at TMI-2 can be considered a kind of common-cause failure, with the systems' failures that initiated the accident in turn triggering a cascade of errors and confusion among the plant operators. Such complex system failures, with operators responding in a manner that worsened the problem rather than solving it, were not anticipated by Rasmussen. (One result of TMI was that training programs for reactor operators in the United States are now considerably more stringent.)

Nonetheless, while the entire accident at TMI-2 was not proposed in the Rasmussen report, many of the individual events of the accident were covered by the report. Within the nuclear power industry, TMI inspired new interest in probabilistic risk-analysis techniques. It was now obvious, however, that the generalized approach of Rasmussen would not be sufficient to predict the future behavior of all reactors in this country. New probabilistic risk analyses would be needed, tailored to individual reactors. In the early 1980s, the NRC began authorizing a series of PRA studies to be performed on reactors across the United States. These studies brought in a wide range of results, showing that the probability of a catastrophic failure varied widely from reactor to reactor. (The original Rasmussen report had concentrated on two actual reactors, a PWR and a BWR.)

For better or worse, the TMI accident had a chilling effect on the development of nuclear power in the United States. The cost of building and insuring a reactor soared, and the power industry rapidly began to lose interest in building new nuclear reactors.

Then, just as the storm over the Three Mile Island accident might have showed some signs of abating, a far worse nuclear accident occurred, a genuine meltdown that released radioactive elements into both the atmosphere and the groundwater, about as close to a worst-case nuclear accident as can be expected in this century. But this accident was not in Pennsylvania or even in the United States. It took place half a world away, in the Soviet Union, in a small town previously unknown to most people in the West: Chernobyl.

Human error may have greatly exacerbated the accident at the TMI-2 reactor, but it was the cause of the accident at Chernobyl. The meltdown at Chernobyl was caused by deliberate, unauthorized experimentation by the operators of the reactor.

On April 25, 1986, the operators of the nuclear plant at Chernobyl began testing their reactor to see how much energy it could continue to produce in an emergency situation. Toward this end, they began adjusting the power on the reactor outside of the range in which it was supposed to be working, a process reporter Christopher Flavin calls "running the reactor by the seat of their pants rather than the operating manual."[18] By 1:23 on the morning of April 26, the operators had pushed the reactor into an extremely unstable state, although apparently they were unaware of this. Unbeknownst to them, the reactor core began to melt.

When the heat level of the reactor began to rise precipitously, the operators pressed the emergency button, but the control rods, which had been removed from the reactor for the test, could not be reinserted in time. Within four and a half seconds, the power level of the reactor rose 2,000 times—a "slow nuclear explosion," in Flavin's words. The fuel rods were torn apart. The water circulating throughout the core turned instantly to steam, and the resulting steam explosion blew open the concrete containment. Hydrogen formed through chemical reactions in the core. Air rushed into the reactor, mixing with the hydrogen; two or three seconds later, this volatile mixture created a second explosion, propelling molten radioactive materials into the night and setting the building on fire.

Brave fire fighters mounted a battle against the flames although they knew they were exposing themselves to high levels of radiation. Fifty workers at the plant received massive doses of radiation, and twenty-nine of them died of radiation sickness. More than 200 other people received dangerously high levels of radiation and may well develop cancer some years in the future.

What makes the accident at Chernobyl more frightening still is that there was an actual release of radioactive material into the environment, both into the groundwater and into the atmosphere. Not long after the accident, increased atmospheric radiation levels were detected in Eastern Europe.

Word of the accident spread slowly through the clumsy Soviet bureaucracy. Combined with the natural Soviet tendency to throw a cloak of secrecy over controversial matters, this led to a slow but dawning awareness of the accident in the West. Over the course of days, the story leaked out of the USSR. It was not until the fall of 1986, however, that the full story was known, when the Soviets presented a remarkably thorough and vivid report of the accident to scientists and reporters around the world.

What are the larger implications of the accident at Chernobyl? Will cancer levels in Europe and the Soviet Union rise as a result of the accident?

We may never know. It's impossible to tell the source of a given case of cancer, and it will be many years before there is a significant rise in general cancer levels due to Chernobyl, if indeed there is any rise at all.

Perhaps the most common question on the lips of American observers was: Can it happen here? Opponents of nuclear power were quick to point to Chernobyl as an example of the kind of accident that they had long feared at nuclear plants in the United States, but these fears may not be well founded. The reactor at Chernobyl was of a type rarely used in the West—only one major U.S. reactor is of this type, and it is used for the creation of fuel for nuclear weapons, not for energy generation—and the containment around the reactor was extremely fragile; in fact, there was no containment at all in the sense that the term is used for U.S. reactors. Even if such an accident could occur at a nuclear power plant in the United States, there is every reason to believe that the containment would prevent the spread of radioactive materials.

What does the Chernobyl accident say about the predictive abilities of probabilistic risk analysis? Alas, not much. Few if any such analyses have been performed on plants of the Chernobyl variety, although it was known long before the accident at Chernobyl that this type of reactor was unstable and subject to unpredictable performance. WASH-1400 never even mentioned this type of reactor.

■ ■ ■

The jury is still out on probabilistic risk analysis for nuclear reactors. Supporters of the technique argue that it is better to have even limited, probabilistic knowledge of the future behavior of this technology system than none at all. Opponents believe that risk analysis lulls us into a dangerous complacency by making us think that we understand our technology better than we actually do. But even as the controversy over the use of PRA in the nuclear industry continues, the techniques of PRA have begun to be adopted in other fields of technology. One of these is the chemical-processing industry, as we shall see in the next chapter.

PART THREE
OTHER RISKY SYSTEMS

PREDICTING

EIGHT

CHEMICAL
TECHNOLOGIES

In the early hours of Monday morning, December 3, 1984, the city of Bhopal, India, erupted with the sounds of gasping, choking, and pain. In the slums and shantytowns of the city's industrial area, where poor people live in shacks, tents, or on the sidewalks or open ground, a vicious cloud of chemicals moved through the night like the Angel of Death, awakening its unsuspecting victims with a sudden, terrifying onslaught.

The chemicals in the cloud attacked both the nervous systems of its victims and the mucous membranes of the eyes and lungs. Their lungs filled with fluid secretions that strangled them. The suffocating victims of the attack fled into the darkness, only to discover that there was no place to flee.

It wasn't hard for the population to figure out where the chemical cloud was coming from. Many of the poor people awakened suddenly in the night lived in the shadow of the Union Carbide chemical plant, and they had known that such a thing was possible, even if they had believed it unlikely. To escape the cloud they ran away from the plant, not realizing that this was the very direction in which the wind was pushing the cloud.

By morning the cloud had dissipated, but in its wake it had left a scene of horror. Thousands of people were dead. Tens of thousands were crushed into the crowded city hospital, where there was barely room for them to stand and scarcely enough personnel to treat them. Stacks of corpses stood in the street, waiting for the government to dispose of them. Men, women, and children stumbled through the streets, searching for their loved ones or crying for the loss of those they already knew to be dead.

No one really knows what the death count was at Bhopal. The official government figure was 2,000 dead, but this was almost certainly an underestimate. Subsequent investigations place the figure at anywhere from 5,000 to 10,000. Perhaps as many as 60,000 people suffered from lung or nervous-system damage.

How could such a thing happen? As with the nuclear accidents discussed in the last chapter, the answer is human error, the factor that makes technological accidents so much more likely to occur than they ought to be.

■ ■ ■

Nuclear technology deals in the fundamental stuff of matter, the particles that make up the atom. The power in the atom is great, but there is danger there as well.

The stuff in which the chemical industry deals is not quite so fundamental, but the risks are at least as great, as the accident at Bhopal clearly illustrates. Chemical processing deals not in the particles that make up atoms but in the atoms themselves, and in the structures called molecules that are formed when atoms bind their electron shells to one another.

For the most part, chemical technology deals in the type of molecules that chemists refer to as *organic molecules*, complex structures of atoms based around the atoms of the element carbon. Carbon is a "friendly" element; it combines easily and in a number of different ways with other atoms. Molecules based on the element carbon can be large and complex. The term "organic molecules" refers to the fact that living organisms are made almost entirely of large and complex carbon-based molecules, although carbon-based molecules are also found outside of living organisms. That a molecule is organic doesn't mean that it was once part of an organism.

Many molecules, both organic and inorganic, have commercial uses; hence, the production of such molecules is an industry in itself, one performed in giant vats at large plants around the world. The uses of such molecules are too many and too varied to be listed here, but suffice it to say that some of these molecules, such as those used in insecticides and herbicides, can be deadly to living creatures. Indeed, it is this very deadliness that gives these molecules their value.

The Union Carbide plant at Bhopal was manufacturing a number of different chemical pesticides and herbicides. To manufacture these chemicals, a number of intermediate chemicals are first produced, then combined with one another to produce the final chemical products. These intermediate chemicals are commonly stored in large tanks outside the plant while waiting for further processing. One of the chemicals stored outside the Union Carbide plant was methyl isocyanate, MIC for short.

MIC is a deadly poison. A report entitled "The Health Effects of Methyl Isocyanate, Cyanide and Monomethylamine Exposure" by an organization called the National Resources Defense Council, published as an appendix to the book *The Bhopal Tragedy* by Ward Morehouse and M. Arun Subramaniam, cites the following immediate effects of MIC exposure, as observed at Bhopal:

> vomiting
> foreign-body sensation in eyes
> diarrhea
> whiteness in the eye
> swelling of legs
> frothing at the mouth
> palpitations
> headache and giddiness
> vomiting of blood
> sore throat
> severe chest congestion
> weakness of tongue and limbs
> pain and burning sensation in the chest
> paralysis
> coughing and breathlessness
> stupor
> chills
> coma
> cold/clammy skin
> fever[19]

In addition, MIC apparently has long-term effects, including breathlessness or choking, respiratory alkalosis, chest pain, "altered consciousness," bronchoalvola lavage, central airway obstruction, vomiting, muscular weakness, impaired O_2 uptake, low vital capacity, and fibrosis in lung biopsies.[20]

A chemical this deadly should be kept in a highly secure location, with stringent safety measures to prevent it from escaping into the environment. And, indeed, the Union Carbide company at Bhopal had taken precautions against the escape of the MIC stored in a tank outside the plant. Yet, one by one, all of the safety precautions fell by the wayside, and the chemical escaped into the atmosphere as a gas. The chain of events leading to the release is astonishing in itself, because by all odds the probabilities against such a sequence of events must be huge, at least in a properly maintained installation.

On the evening of December 2, 1984, a few hours before the gas release, workers were performing routine maintenance on the MIC production unit. One worker was flushing out several pipelines with water. These pipelines were connected to a relief valve vent header (RVVH), a separate pipeline designed to carry any toxic gases created in the MIC tank and channel them to the vent gas scrubber (VGS), a device intended to neutralize such gases before they could enter the atmosphere.

The RVVH was, in turn, connected to the MIC tank. Because water can combine explosively with MIC to produce a deadly gas, it was important that the water being used to flush the pipes not be allowed to enter the RVVH, from which it could spread to the MIC tank. To prevent it from doing so, the worker closed the valve that connected the pipes with the RVVH. Unfortunately, he failed to seal the valve tightly with a device called a slipbind, so that it was still possible for water to force its way through. Apparently, the need for the slipbind had been omitted from the maintenance manuals for the plant.

Worse, a new pipe had recently been installed in the MIC tanks. This pipe, called a jumper line, also carried gases from the MIC tank to the VGS, by way of a line called the process vent header, or PVH. Both the jumper line and the RVVH provided routes by which water could find its way from the pipes being flushed into the MIC tank.

This is apparently what happened, although the precise details are difficult to reconstruct. Water found its way through this complex welter of pipes into the tank; about 50 gallons (200 liters) of it poured into the MIC. Gas formed inside the tank. Ordinarily, deadly gases formed inside the tank are channeled through the RVVH and into the VGS, where they are neutralized. And in fact, the gases *were* channeled into the VGS—but the VGS wasn't working. (There is considerable dispute as to *why* the VGS wasn't working. Some have argued that the VGS malfunctioned and failed to release the caustic soda that it used to neutralize the gas; others said that the mechanism had been dismantled and could not be put back together in time to stop the accident.)

From the VGS the gas entered the environment through an overflow valve. No more safety devices stood in its way. As of 12:30 on the morning of December 3, the gas was on the loose, and the tragedy was under way.

And yet, as late as 12:30, it might still have been

possible to stop the catastrophe. Workers had noticed suspicious activity around the tank, and supervisors had been alerted, but they postponed further investigation until after their scheduled 12:30 tea break. By the time tea was over, it was much too late. The workers were driven back by the very gas that they had inadvertently created.

■ ■ ■

Much like the incident at TMI-2, the Bhopal tragedy was the result not of a single accident but of a series of accidents, and all of these accidents were, to one degree or another, the result of human error.

The jumper line should never have been installed in the MIC tank. The worker should have placed a slipbind on the RVVH valve. The VGS should have been operative. The workers and their supervisors should not have postponed their investigation until after the tea break.

None of these things *should* have happened, and if any *one* of them hadn't happened, the accident probably would never have taken place. An event tree for the Bhopal catastrophe would doubtlessly show tremendous odds against it. The accident is made more frightening still by the fact that similar accidents have been narrowly averted before and after the Bhopal tragedy, under similar circumstances. Not long after Bhopal, in fact, a similar gas release took place at the Union Carbide plant in West Virginia, but with far less tragic results.

In fact, accidental releases of deadly gas are fairly common but in most instances do not result in wholesale death and destruction. In Bhopal, however, conditions were perfect for tragedy. Weather conditions were right. Crowds of the homeless and semi-homeless clustered about the plant. All that was needed was a supply of deadly chemicals, which was provided by the MIC tank at Union Carbide.

■ ■ ■

Perhaps for its own defense, the chemical industry has become increasingly interested over the last decade in the techniques of probabilistic risk analysis. The fault tree in Figure 8.1[21] is taken from a report published in 1978. It uses somewhat different symbols from the fault trees we studied in Chapter Four, but the meaning is fairly clear. It shows the various paths that might lead to a "major fire, explosion, or detonation" at a chemical plant and was created as part of an actual chemical-plant safety review by R. M. Stewart and G. Hensley in England. The top event—the accident itself—is on the left-hand side of the tree rather than the top.

Will the techniques of probabilistic risk analysis lead to a safer future in the chemical industry? Perhaps, though this is by no means certain. It is difficult to escape the notion that no predictive techniques could have prevented the accident at Bhopal because of the dominant role played by human error. Risk analysis can pinpoint the need for safety systems and suggest which safety systems we are better off using. But human beings will always be capable of defeating safety systems, either through willful disregard or pure stupidity.

Nonetheless, knowledge is always better than ignorance, and risk analysis can show the chemical industry where its problems lie, even if it can't always point out a surefire way to cure them.

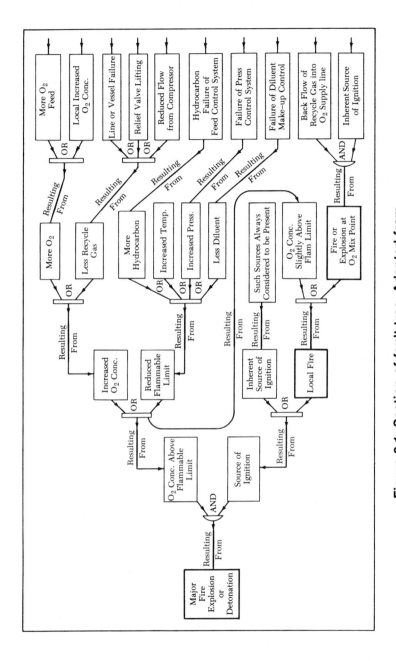

Figure 8.1. Section of fault tree. Adapted from G. M. Kinchin et al., "Plant Reliability and Safety."

■ ■ ■

Are there other areas of technology that might benefit from risk analysis? Of course. In fact, there are probably few areas of technology that couldn't benefit.

In the next chapter, we'll look at a relatively new technology with a small but recognized component of risk; we'll examine some of the risks involved and some of the potential disasters that may take place.

Most importantly, however, we will learn a lesson about the psychology of risk assessment and perhaps catch a glimpse of some deeper reasons why probabilistic risk analysis is controversial.

PREDICTING

NINE

THE TECHNOLOGY
OF LIFE

As we mentioned in the last chapter, living organisms are made of large and complex molecules, built around the element carbon. Your own body, the fabulously complicated and sophisticated organism that is even now holding and reading this book, is constructed almost entirely of these organic molecules. They provide not only the bricks and scaffolding of your skin and bones but the machinery that allows you to live, breathe, digest food, run, talk, and even think.

How can we compare molecules to machinery? If you could see inside the cells of your body and watch the activity that takes place there on a microscopic level, you would see a bevy of "machines" at work that would put an urban construction site to shame. These "machines," darting frantically about the interior of the cell performing their individual tasks, are called *enzymes*, and all of them are of particular types of carbon-based molecules known as *proteins*. Each of these "machines"—these molecules—is a single strand of atoms, twisted back on itself into an intricate shape appropriate to the job that it has been assigned to perform within the cell.

And who assigns jobs to these molecules? Who is the foreman of all this activity within the cell? The answer lies inside a tightly guarded chamber at the center of the cell called the *nucleus*. Within the nucleus of every cell of your body—and, for that matter, every living cell of every living creature on this planet—lies a collection of molecules called *chromosomes*, made of yet another carbon-based substance known as *deoxyribonucleic acid*, DNA for short. If the enzymes in the cell are machines, then the DNA molecules are a library. They contain all the information necessary to build and operate a living organism. Through a complex series of chemical reactions, they use this information to control the activity of the cell.

More precisely, the DNA contains the "recipes" for the enzymes that do the actual work in the cell. Whenever the cell requires a new enzyme, the chromosomes (and the enzymes that aid the chromosomes in their work) initiate a process that leads to the construction of the required molecules. The chromosomes in the cells of your body contain the library of chemical formulas that make your body go.

The DNA library may well be the most important repository of information on earth. If it were possible to read this information, we could tap into the deepest secrets of life itself. And if we could rewrite this information, we would have a powerful tool that might well allow us to cure disease and even alter the human organism itself.

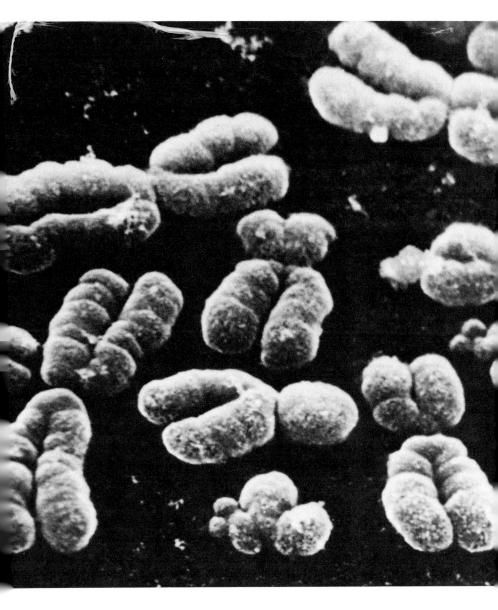

Highly magnified view of chromosomes

In the early 1970s, we gained both of these abilities. We can not only read the information on the chromosomes—the so-called genetic information—but we can also rewrite it, at least in simple organisms such as bacteria. In addition, considerable progress has been made in recent years on rewriting the chromosomes of laboratory mice.

But with these abilities comes not only tremendous power but the possibility of tremendous danger. So it is significant that the scientific community of the 1970s, faced with one of the most powerful advances in the history of biology, paused for several years to assess the risks of the new technology it had created.

■ ■ ■

Recombinant DNA *technology* is a set of techniques for editing the chromosomes of the single-celled organisms called bacteria and inserting new genetic information, often taken from the chromosomes of human beings. This not only gives us a technique for studying the information in these chromosomes—learning what chemicals the chromosomes contain information for and under what circumstances the chemicals are produced—but it provides us with a method of manufacturing unlimited supplies of certain useful organic chemicals, such as insulin and human growth hormone. Thus, recombinant DNA techniques are valuable not only to scientists but to industry.

The most common bacterium into which human and other chromosomes are "spliced" is *Escherichia coli*. *E. coli*, as it is more commonly known, is a benevolent bacterium found in great quantities in the human intestines; there is at least a pound of *E. coli* in your guts right now, helping you to digest your last meal. *E. coli* was the first bacterium to have its

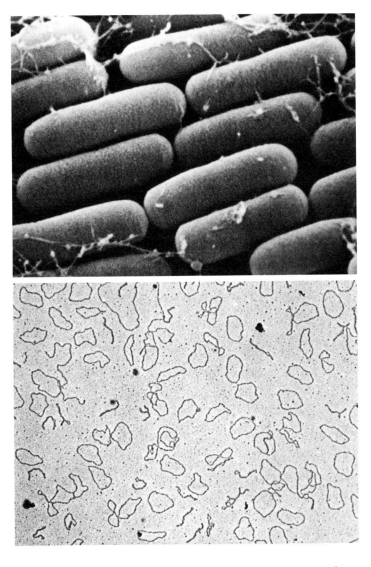

Top: E. coli, *the type of bacteria most commonly used in recombinant DNA research. Bottom: plasmids, circular strands of bacterial DNA into which foreign genes are "spliced" in genetic engineering experiments.*

chromosomes fully analyzed by biologists and therefore was a natural for recombinant DNA techniques, simply by virtue of its familiarity.

The recombinant DNA techniques were developed by a handful of biologists in the early 1970s. But one of these biologists, Paul Berg, stopped to wonder if maybe this new gene-splicing technology might not have a darker side.

What, for instance, if a biologist were to splice a chromosome from a smallpox virus into an *E. coli* bacterium? Probably, the resulting hybrid organism would be completely harmless, but what if it turned out to combine the infective power of smallpox with the penchant of *E. coli* for seeking out human intestines? The result might be a disease-causing bacterium of unprecedented virulence. If it escaped the laboratory and multiplied, it might create an epidemic that could wipe out millions of lives.

Berg immediately voiced his concerns to a group of his fellow biologists, who then produced a letter and distributed it within the scientific community. Soon, Berg and his colleagues had organized a conference of most of the major figures in molecular biology, the branch of science that studies the molecules of which living organisms are made. The conference was held in Pacific Grove, California, at the Asilomar Conference Center; thus it became known as the Asilomar Conference.

The Asilomar Conference was a milestone in the history of science and technology. It may well have been the first time that the developers of a new technology made a concerted attempt to assess the risks of a technology before it was even fully developed. Instead of plunging headlong into the development of systems that contained an unknown level of risk, the molecular biologists at Asilomar made an honest attempt to decide if the risks involved in recombinant DNA technology were worth the benefits—and what, if anything, should be done to contain those risks.

And yet the results of the Asilomar Conference were disheartening, not because of the attempt on the part of the biologists to assess the risks of their new technology but because of the public reaction to that attempt.

The overall assessment of the biologists at Asilomar was that the risk of recombinant DNA technology was relatively small. In fact, when a biologist breaks apart the chromosomes of, say, a smallpox virus and studies them separately, he or she has probably *lessened* the risk associated with the chromosomes. Thus, gene splicing probably entailed a smaller risk than traditional biological techniques for studying viral organisms in petri dishes.

Nonetheless, there was a certain measure of risk involved. Probabilistic techniques were not used, so it is difficult to measure the precise degree of risk. And so the biologists agreed to perform their experiments in special containment chambers, under the direction of the National Institutes of Health. In all probability, the precautions taken by the biologists were much greater than the risks involved with recombinant DNA experimentation warranted.

And yet, when nonscientists read about the biologists' attempts to assess the risks of this new technology, the general assumption was that the risks must be huge indeed, if scientists were willing to go to this much trouble to assess them. Many people honestly believed that the Asilomar Conference was an attempt to cover up the risks of this frightening new technology rather than understand them. Gene-splicing technology conjured up visions of strange organisms created in the laboratory, hideous new diseases striking down the population. The public was in favor of putting restrictions on recombinant DNA technology far stricter than those advocated by the scientists. Many people wanted to abandon the technology altogether.

This, in turn, created a backlash in the scientific community. Many biologists who had willingly come forward at the conference to discuss their fears about the new technology became wary of speaking to reporters, or even other scientists, about the slightest possibility of risk in their work. The scientists and the public became polarized, each fearing that the other had their worst interests in mind.

This may be the greatest irony of risk assessment. If we are to have an advanced technology on this planet, it is important that we understand the risks of that technology. We must analyze that risk with whatever tools are at hand, to produce as precise an assessment as we are capable of making. And we must use that analysis to make technology safer, so that we will not destroy ourselves in the attempt to master our environment.

But the scientists and engineers and, yes, industries that create that technology are often afraid to admit that there is any risk involved at all, for fear that the public will overreact and demand that we turn our back on technology once and for all. And the public correctly sees that scientists, engineers, and industries are not being completely honest in their discussions of risk, which leads to a perception that the risks are much greater than they are made out to be.

If we are to properly foresee the risks of our technology and be able to predict technological disasters so as to avoid them, there must be a bridge of trust between those who build the technology and those who are ostensibly its beneficiaries. In recent years, this trust has broken down, leading to a tendency on the part of those who build nuclear reactors and chemical plants and other risky systems to downplay the risks of those systems and a tendency on the part of the public to overreact to the risks.

Is technology worth the risks involved? The answer would seem to be a qualified yes. It is much too late for the human race to turn its collective back on the benefits of an advanced technology. But it is also important that we make our technologies as safe as they can be, and that requires some sort of advanced method of risk assessment. Until something better comes along, probabilistic risk analysis may be the best method we have.

As long as there is technology, there will be technological disasters. But there were natural disasters—disease, famine, earthquakes—long before there were technological disasters. It is technology that stands between us and natural disasters; as long as we have a choice of disasters, perhaps we are better off with those over which we have *some* control.

NOTES

1. Norman C. Rasmussen et al., *Reactor Safety Study*, WASH-1400 (Washington, DC: Nuclear Regulatory Commission, 1975), Appendix II, p. 18.
2. "Nuclear Energy," *The New Book of Popular Science*, vol. 2 (New York: Grolier, 1987), p. 366.
3. Ibid., p. 366.
4. Rasmussen et al., p. 6.
5. Ibid., p. 6.
6. Ibid., Executive Summary, p. 8.
7. Ibid., Executive Summary, p. 9.
8. Ibid., Executive Summary, p. 12.
9. Ibid., p. 55.
10. Ibid., p. 56.
11. Ibid., Appendix I, p. 48ff.
12. Ibid., Appendix II, p. 19.
13. Ibid., p. 50.
14. Henry W. Kendall, *The Risks of Nuclear Power Reactors: A Review of the NRC Reactor Safety Study WASH-1400*,

NUREG-75/014 (Cambridge, Mass.: Union of Concerned Scientists, 1977).

15. John G. Kemeny et al., *Report of the President's Commission on the Accident at Three Mile Island* (Washington, DC: U.S. Government Printing Office, 1979), p. 111.

16. Quoted in Kemeny et al., *Report of the President's Commission on Three Mile Island,* p. 131.

17. N. C. Rasmussen and S. Levine, "Nuclear Plant PRA: How Far Has It Come?", *Risk Analysis,* vol. 4, no. 4, December 1984, p. 248.

18. Christopher Flavin, *Reassessing Nuclear Power: The Fallout from Chernobyl* (Washington, DC: Worldwatch Institute, 1987), p. 41.

19. Ward Morehouse and M. Arun Subramaniam, *The Bhopal Tragedy: What Really Happened and What It Means for American Workers and Communities at Risk* (New York: Council on International and Public Affairs, 1986), pp. 171–72.

20. Ibid., pp. 173–74.

21. G. M. Kinchin and M. Finstp, "Plant Reliability and Safety," *Proceedings of the Seminar on Major Chemical Hazards Held at the Lorch Foundation, 26 and 27 April, 1978* (Oxfordshire, England: Harwell, 1978), p. 173.

22. Raymond F. Boykin, "Risk Analysis for Physical Hazards: A Toxic Chemical Case Study," *Risk Analysis in the Chemical Industry* (Washington, DC: Chemical Manufacturers Association, 1985), p. 221.

23. Ibid., p. 221.

SOURCES USED

Flavin, Christopher. *Reassessing Nuclear Power: The Fallout from Chernobyl.* Washington, DC: Worldwatch Institute, 1987.

Gray, Mike, and Ira Rosen. *The Warning.* New York: W. W. Norton, 1982.

Kemeny, John G., et al. *Report of the President's Commission on the Accident at Three Mile Island.* Washington, DC: U.S. Government Printing Office, 1979.

Kendall, Henry W. *The Risks of Nuclear Power Reactors: A Review of the NRC Reactor Safety Study WASH-1400,* NUREG-75/014. Cambridge, Mass.: Union of Concerned Scientists, 1977.

Marples, David R. *Chernobyl and Nuclear Power in the U.S.S.R.* New York: St. Martin's Press, 1986.

Morehouse, Ward, and M. Arun Subramaniam. *The Bhopal Tragedy: What Really Happened and What It Means for American Workers and Communities at Risk.* New York: Council on International and Public Affairs, 1986.

Perrow, Charles. *Normal Accidents: Living with High Risk Technologies.* New York: Basic Books, 1984.

Rasmussen, Norman C. *Reactor Safety Study,* WASH-1400. Washington, DC: Nuclear Regulatory Commission, 1975.

The New Book of Popular Science, vol. 2. New York: Grolier, 1987.

Proceedings of the Seminar on Major Chemical Hazards Held at the Lorch Foundation, 26 and 27 April, 1978. Oxfordshire, England: Harwell, 1978.

Risk Analysis in the Chemical Industry. Washington, DC: Chemical Manufacturers Association, 1985.

INDEX